Leadership Talk

Leadership Talk

A Discourse Approach to Leader Emergence

Robyn Walker and Jolanta Aritz

First published in 2014 by
Business Expert Press, LLC
222 East 46th Street, New York, NY 10017
www.businessexpertpress.com

ISBN-13: 978-1-60649-708-1 (paperback)
ISBN-13: 978-1-60649-709-8 (e-book)

Business Expert Press Corporate Communication Collection

Collection ISSN: 2156-8162 (print)
Collection ISSN: 2156-8170 (electronic)

Cover and interior design by Exeter Premedia Services Private Ltd.,
Chennai, India

First edition: 2014

10 9 8 7 6 5 4 3 2 1

Printed in the United States of America.

Abstract

Leadership Talk takes an in-depth look at an emerging approach to the study of business leadership that focuses on language as a vehicle for communicating leadership. Traditionally, management theories have taken a psychological approach to leadership, often assuming that it is a personality trait located within an individual. In contrast, the discursive approach to leadership, which is the focus of this book, assumes that leadership is created through communication practices. With this understanding, we explore a new definition of leadership as the expression of ideas in talk or in action that are recognized by others as capable of progressing tasks or solving problems. The practical implication of this view of leadership suggests that leaders must constantly enact and communicate their relationship to their followers in such a way as to be recognized by them as a leader. Leadership thus becomes the negotiation that occurs between potential leaders and followers and is thus created in interaction within a particular organizational culture and context rather than residing in the individual. Consequently, leadership becomes the purview of those with excellent analytical skills and communication practices rather than a given personality type. It can be thus be learned and practiced by anyone with the tools to do so.

This book is intended for a broad audience, including students and professors in business schools as well as practicing business executives and those who aspire to leadership positions. It provides an overview of elements of communication that are involved in the construction of leadership, as well as a discussion of leadership practices and their effect regarding gender and cultural differences. The goal of the book is to inform current and future leaders how to more effectively approach leadership as a communication practice that involves and depends upon the response of potential followers. This is particularly important in today's business environment, which involves diverse participants with differing expectations and values related to the practice of leadership.

Keywords

leadership, discourse studies, discursive leadership, gender and leadership, intercultural leadership, group dynamics and communication, business communication, applied linguistics, management communication

Contents

Preface

This book is intended to introduce practitioners and students of business to the study of discursive leadership. A discursive approach to leadership has some critical differences from the more traditional or psychological approach to leadership with which most of us are familiar. These differences are important to understand if one is to really benefit from the study of a discursive approach, because it requires developing a different way of looking at reality.

To best understand the two different ways of looking at the world that are foundational to the assumptions of both the discursive and psychological leadership approaches, we will take a detour through two different theories of knowledge.

Historically, science as a discipline first looked at phenomena of the natural world. Galileo looked toward the skies to understand the universe, Newton observed falling objects to develop a theory of gravity, and da Vinci dissected corpses to learn about drawing the human anatomy. The natural sciences seek to elucidate the rules that govern the natural world through scientific methods. The scientific method is based on **empiricism**, a theory that assumes that experience or observation alone, often without due regard for system and theory, can help us to describe reality. Empiricism assumes that reality is testable by observations made using our physical senses or using instruments that extend those senses. The human being, in other words, is the ground of knowledge, the center of the universe.

The term *natural science* is used to distinguish that subject from the social sciences, which traditionally have applied the scientific method to study human behavior and social patterns. The use of the methods used by the natural sciences for social-science subjects is called positivism. **Positivism** is a philosophy of science based on the view that information derived from logical and mathematical treatments and reports of sensory experience is the exclusive source of all authoritative knowledge[1] and that there is valid knowledge or truth only in scientific knowledge.[2] This view holds that society, like the physical world, operates according to general laws.

At the turn of the 20th century, however, the first wave of German sociologists formally introduced methodological antipositivism, proposing that social-science research should concentrate on human cultural norms, values, symbols, and social processes viewed from a subjective perspective. **Antipositivism** is the view in social science that the social realm may not be subject to the same methods of investigation as the natural world and that social interactions may not operate as general laws of the universe, like gravity, for instance.

This view was further developed in a sociological theory of knowledge called **social constructionism**, which considers how phenomena or objects of consciousness develop in social contexts. A social construction (also called a social construct) is a concept or practice that is the construct (or artifact) of a particular group. When we say that something is socially constructed, we are focusing on its dependence on contingent variables of our social selves rather than any inherent quality that it possesses in itself, like a stone or a molecule of water.

Social constructionism is typically positioned in opposition to essentialism, which sees phenomena in terms of inherent, transhistorical essences independent of human judgment.[3] In other words, social constructionism assumes that all social behavior is constructed by human practices and may in large part be separated from or somewhat oblivious to the natural laws of the universe. One simple example would be our treatment of body hair. Although, it is natural to have body hair, human cultures have a variety of ways of dealing with it. For example, some cultures shave it, while others don't; similarly, some cultures see it as attractive for a variety of reasons, while others don't. And these values change over time in different ways in different cultures. For example, in the United States, facial hair on men is fashionable during some decades, while in others times, it is not. As this example is intended to show, if humans operated only within natural laws, they would ignore the presence of body hair and accept it as "natural," rather than as a fashion statement.

So what has the positivist or antipositivist view of the world have to do with leadership, you might ask? The answer is that the **psychological approach** to leadership is an outgrowth of the positivist worldview, while the discursive approach is a consequence of the antipositivist view.

In other words, the psychological approach assumes that individuals have an essence that they are born with that largely determines who they are. It therefore also assumes that the individual is separate from society. He or she has the agency to control who he or she "is." Because of this view, the psychological perspective of leadership focuses on the individual and his or her mental or cognitive functions.

In contrast, the **discursive approach** assumes that individuals are to a large degree formed by the social processes around them. The individual and society are thus inseparable. This means that individuals have limited agency in terms of who they might be or become, since a large amount of who they are from the very beginning has been shaped by social practices and values. On the plus side, the individual is not an unchangeable "essence" but is always adapting to and affected by social circumstances to varying degrees. The "glue" that holds this relationship of the individual and society together is communication practices.

Another illustration of the difference between these two approaches might be to say that psychological leadership researchers look at how the individual affects the organization while discursive leadership scholars look at how individuals, groups, and organizations are shaped through language use.

From these assumptions we can see how and why psychological leadership theories have focused on identifying the traits or personality characteristics of the leader and often treat leaders as "personalities." In contrast, discursive leadership scholars look at how talk constructs or designates the leader in an interaction. In this approach, the person with position power may not be the leader who emerges in a specific interaction. The discursive approach focuses on how talk is used to construct the phenomenon of "leadership."

To thus benefit from the discussion in this text, it is important to question some of your assumptions about reality and to attempt to begin viewing reality from the social constructionist view, if you already don't. (This topic will be discussed in more detail in Chapter 1.) This book includes some discussion of issues related to leadership from the psychological perspective to complement the discussion of the discursive approach.

Although much of the book focuses on communication and the use of language, it is designed for those who do not have a background in linguistics and its many subfields. It is not intended to provide such a foundation but is instead intended to make available to business practitioners and students some of the valuable insights of this discipline. For that reason, it does not provide a discussion of linguistics as a formal discipline or comprehensive coverage of its many facets.

The first chapter of this book introduces the concept of leadership and reviews the major theories of leadership that have come out of a traditional approach to the topic. It also explains the social construction of reality theory and the discursive approach to leadership in more detail.

Chapter 2 identifies and illustrates some key elements of talk with the goal of providing an introduction to discursive leadership as well as providing tools for analyzing and practicing different aspects of talk involved in leadership emergence.

Chapter 3 illustrates the elements of three different leadership styles commonly used in the United States and discusses how the perception of expertise can complicate the emergence of a leader within a group.

Chapter 4 opens with a discussion of a key function of leadership, creating organizational realities, and then explores how talk is used to manage various leadership responsibilities, including conducting performance appraisals, maintaining relationships, facilitating meetings, and managing conflict.

Chapter 5 discusses the challenges of working with those of different cultures and explores how differing leadership styles may affect the contribution and participation of group or team members from various cultures.

Chapter 6 looks at gender and how female leaders are often caught in a double bind. It discusses the elements of stereotypically gendered talk and how analyzing communities of practice can help men and women leaders overcome gender stereotypes.

Chapter 7 reviews some of the ways that those who are or aspire to become leaders can prepare themselves to better apply the concepts explored in this text. It closes with an introduction to nonverbal communication, an important element of communication not addressed in a linguistic approach, but one that is critical for successful leader enactment.

CHAPTER 1

Introduction to Discursive Leadership

A genuine leader is not a searcher for consensus but a molder of consensus.
—Martin Luther King, Jr.

This chapter will introduce you to the field of discursive leadership. Before doing so, however, it is helpful to begin with a shared definition of leadership to provide a ground of understanding from which we can build the discussion that follows. This chapter will also summarize what might be called traditional theories of leadership that have emerged from the management discipline. Again, having a shared understanding of how the field of leadership has developed to date is important for distinguishing how discursive leadership differs from dominant understandings of leadership. It will thus potentially deepen our understandings of the concept of leadership.

What Is Leadership?

Leadership is defined as the ability to influence a group toward the achievement of goals.[1] The emphasis on influence helps us to better understand the differences between leadership and management. While leaders influence people, managers coordinate and organize activities. Table 1.1 illustrates the differences between management and leadership in terms of these functions.

The distinction between management and leadership is an important one because it reveals an opportunity for anyone interested in developing his or her influence potential: that is, anyone can become a leader with the proper understanding of the role and the needed skill set grounded in the ability to influence.

Table 1.1 Functions of management and leadership

Management	Leadership
Produces order and consistency	*Produces change and movement*
Planning and budgeting	Establishing direction
• Establish agendas	• Create a vision
• Set timetables	• Clarify the big picture
• Allocate resources	• Set strategies
Organizing and staffing	Aligning people
• Provide structure	• Communicate goals
• Make job placements	• Seek commitment
• Establish rules and procedures	• Build teams and coalitions
Controlling and problem solving	Motivating and inspiring
• Develop incentives	• Inspire and energize
• Generate creative solutions	• Empower subordinates
• Take corrective action	• Satisfy unmet needs

Source: Adapted from Kotter (1990). pp. 3–8.

In other words, leaders often differ from managers in terms of the type of power they may wield. Managers are appointed; they have legitimate power or what is sometimes called "position power," which enables them to reward and punish employees. The formal authority given to them by their position within an organization gives them the potential to influence employees. Leaders, on the other hand, may be appointed or may emerge. In the latter case, they have the opportunity to influence others beyond the formal authority assigned to them within an organization. Table 1.2 identifies the differing bases of power that arise in groups and organizations.

Of these bases of power, the first three are typically conferred on an individual by an institution or organization. They are the types of power that managers often have been assigned based on their role within an organizational hierarchy.

Ideally, managers would also have the ability to gain the last three types of power listed in the table: referent, expert, and informational power. However, those without formal organizational power also have the opportunity to influence others as leaders, using these three bases of power. Leaders can influence others through their credibility,

Table 1.2 Six bases of power

Basis of power	Definition
Reward power	The capability of controlling the distribution of rewards given or offered to the target.
Coercive power	The capacity to threaten and punish those who do not comply with requests or demands.
Legitimate power	Authority that derives from the power holder's legitimate right to require and demand obedience.
Referent power	Influence based on the target's identification with, attraction to, or respect for the power holder.
Expert power	Influence based on the target's belief that the power holder possesses superior skills and abilities.
Informational power	Influence based on the potential use of informational resources, including rational argument, persuasion, and factual data.

Source: French and Raven (1959).

relationships, knowledge, and expertise—in short, their communication abilities, since all of these elements are established through communication practices. This ability to influence derives from one's ability to be perceived by others as likeable, knowledgeable, and skilled. Most of us view these abilities as being located within an individual. However, there is an alternate way of understanding where the perception of these abilities derives. This alternate way of understanding "reality," if you will, will be discussed later in this chapter as a preface to understanding discursive leadership. But before moving to that discussion, a brief review of traditional views of leadership will be provided, which will help to illustrate the difference between this perspective and the discursive one.

Opportunity to Reflect

With an understanding of the difference between management and leadership, how might this knowledge affect your communication practices if you aim to be seen as a leader in your organization or career field?

Traditional Approaches to Leadership

Broadly speaking, management theories have taken a psychological approach to leadership, which simply means that we assume the substance "leadership" is located within or is an attribute of an individual. This perspective makes sense to most of us because of the focus in western civilization on the individual and his or her development, which has culminated in the intense individualistic values that characterize much of U.S. culture. In other words, this view of leadership is part of our history and culture and thus seems "normal," "natural," or apparent to us.

This psychological assumption about the basis of leadership as a kind of substance located within the individual has been explored by management scholars since the 1930s and has resulted in what may be viewed as four broad categories of leadership theory. What characterizes all of them to a large degree is the assumption that the substance of leadership resides in the individual. These categories are trait, behavioral, contingency, and neocharismatic theories, which are briefly reviewed in the following sections.

Trait Theories

Trait theories assume that leaders demonstrate certain traits, such as charisma, enthusiasm, courage, honesty, self-confidence, and intelligence. The underlying assumption of these approaches, as mentioned previously, is that leadership is located within the personality, social, physical, and intellectual attributes of the individual. Most studies of this type have focused on identifying those attributes, but these efforts have met with certain obstacles. For example, a review of 20 different studies identified nearly 80 leadership traits but found that only five of these traits were common to four or more of the investigations.[2] From this conclusion, it is apparent that the perception of leadership is highly variable; in other words, leadership as a recognized construct is something that is perceived by individuals observing or assessing the supposed leader, and individuals have, to some degree, differing ideas about what leadership is.

The problem with trait theories as such is that if we ignore this variability and focus solely on the traits that are held in common among them, the risk is that we might arrive at a theory of leadership that is too reductionist, that is, it overlooks many of the characteristics that might be perceived as a sign of leadership capability by individuals within an organization. What might be said then based on this approach to leadership is that the findings thus far have led to the conclusion that some traits increase the likelihood of success as a leader, but none guarantee it.[3] Even with the limitations of this approach to understanding leadership, a renewed interest in trait theories has more recently emerged within the management field.

Behavioral Theories

The challenge that was revealed in the attempt to identify universal leadership traits by trait theorists led researchers to look at another aspect of leadership: behavior. The primary benefit of the behavioral approach to leadership was the view that leaders might be trained as opposed to the assumption that leaders are born, not made. A number of studies have looked into the issue of leadership as a set of behaviors rather than as a particular personality style. In general, though, the behavioral approach proposes that leadership is composed of two general kinds of behaviors: task behaviors and relationship behaviors. Task behaviors help group members achieve their objectives and goals, while relationship behaviors help subordinates feel valued and comfortable with each other and the situation. The central focus of the behavioral approach is to identify how leaders can combine these two dimensions to influence others in their efforts to reach a goal.

The behavioral approach does not provide a clear set of prescriptions for leaders but reminds leaders that they should consider how their behaviors affect others on a task and relationship level. One limitation of the behavioral approach is that researchers have been focused on identifying a universal style of leadership, much like trait theorists, and because of the situational element at the core of this approach, this goal has not been attained.

Contingency or Situational Theories

Because of the limitations of both trait and behavioral approaches to leadership, researchers began to focus more on situational influences. The aim of researchers thus became to identify the leadership approach that best matched different situations. In other words, the assumption for leaders is that they must adapt their style to the demands of the situation. Situational leadership stresses that leadership is composed of two dimensions: directive and supportive, which builds on the assumptions developed by behavioral theorists. This means that leaders should change the degree to which they are directive or supportive, depending on the changing needs of employees, the situation, or both. More specifically, the leader should match his or her style to the competence and commitment of employees. For example, if a leader is working with a group with a low skill level, he or she might need to be more directive. If the group is highly skilled and motivated, the leader may not need to provide a great deal of direction but instead should focus on creating an environment where employees feel valued and recognized for their contribution.

There have been a number of criticisms of contingency or situational theories and most have to do with the inability to directly correlate employee behavior to those of the leader. Still, this approach is widely used in organizational training sessions because of its focus on leader flexibility and the unique needs of employees.

Neocharismatic or Transformational Theories

A more recent approach to leadership looks at it in what might be described as "layperson's" terms in that it stresses symbolic and emotionally appealing leadership behaviors and pays less attention to constructing complicated theoretical models. Transformational leadership emerged as an important approach in 1978 when James MacGregor Burns attempted to link the roles of leadership with followership by claiming that leadership is different from power because it is inseparable from followers' needs.[4] In attempting to clarify this definition, he distinguished between two types of leadership: transactional and transformational. Transactional leadership refers to most leadership models in which the ability is viewed as an exchange between the leader and his or her followers. The leader guides or motivates followers in the direction of established goals by clarifying role and task requirements. In contrast, in transformational leadership a person engages with others and creates a connection that raises morale and the level of motivation. This type of leader is attentive to the needs and motives of followers and tries to help them reach their fullest potential.

Charismatic leadership is another area of leadership discussion that emerged at about the same time as Burns' writing. In his theory of charismatic leadership, House suggested that leaders act in unique ways that have specific charismatic effects on their followers.[5] Personal characteristics of a charismatic leader include being dominant, having a strong desire to influence others, being self-confident, and having a strong sense of one's own moral values. In addition to exhibiting specific personality traits, charismatic leaders demonstrate certain types of behaviors. They are strong role models for the beliefs and values they want their followers to adopt. They are competent and communicate high expectations. They also arouse task-relevant motives in followers that may include affiliation, power, and esteem. Transformational leaders set out to employ followers and to nurture them in exchange.

Like other streams of theoretical development, however, transformational leadership approaches have come under criticism for a number of reasons, including a lack of conceptual clarity and resulting difficulty in measurement.

Opportunity to Reflect

What theories of leadership have you applied in your career or seen applied by others? What elements were successful? Which were not so successful? Why?

The Language Turn and How It Changes Our Understanding of Leadership

What distinguishes traditional management approaches to leadership and the discursive approach addressed in this text, is how we view reality. This concern with perception of reality has traditionally been assigned to the discipline of philosophy and thus can be off putting to many because it is often viewed as having little practical application. However, our assumptions about the nature of reality have a dramatic effect on our understanding of the world, how it operates, and our role and potential to act within it. The concept therefore has enormous implications for our understanding of leadership and how it manifests within an organizational setting.

In the next section we will examine an alternate way of understanding reality that differs from the one at the basis of traditional leadership theories. The discussion will begin with a brief explanation of how this alternate view of reality emerged, what that alternate view assumes, and how the alternate perspective affects our practice of leadership.

What Is the Social Construction of Reality?

The emergence of a discursive approach to leadership is in part due to what has been called the "linguistic turn." The linguistic turn considers that language is not used to make an accurate representation of reality if reality is defined as internal or external worlds that existed before our ability to use language. In other words, language is weighted in culture and thus carries values and meanings that reside in and are an outgrowth of culture. Our understanding of reality is already filtered through a lens laden with the values of our culture. Because of this, some hold that we cannot have an understanding of the world that exists without or before language. We do not have access to the natural world in a direct way. This assumption has been questioned by some, but that is beyond the scope of this text. What is helpful about this understanding is the power of language in constructing what we perceive to be real.

The social construction view contradicts what many of us have been taught to believe: The world exists independent of human meaning-making activities. That is, we believe that we can know reality as it exists apart from us. Scholars working from a social constructionist perspective, however, argue that it is impossible for human beings to be objective. We cannot divorce ourselves from our values, beliefs, and experiences in order to see the world as it is. Instead, we perceive and interpret the world through the lens of our worldview and our experiences. To put it another way, we make meaning based on our values, beliefs, and life experiences. We are subjective, not objective, beings.

The important point to glean from this perspective is the significance of the activity of meaning-making in interpreting as well as creating and reinforcing existing views of our reality. Meaning-making is the process of communication. Communication is the process of exchanging information and meaning between or among individuals through a system of symbols, signs, and behaviors. Even in situations in which we do not share a common system, we still will make meaning based on our own perceptual lens or meaning-making system. We experience and view the outside world and then interpret what is out there based on our current knowledge base, which includes experiences, values, and beliefs. Using a psychological term, we project ourselves—all that we are in terms of our cultural understanding and personal experiences—onto the outside world.

This perceptual process underscores the opportunities and obstacles embedded in the process of communication. Let's look at an example using the issue of global warming. There are a variety of views on this issue, as listed below:

- Global warming exists. It is created by human beings. Therefore, human beings can do something to stop it.
- Global warming exists. It is created by human beings. Even though human beings may be able to do something to stop it, that isn't a good idea because it may affect our current way of life.
- Global warming does not exist. What we are seeing is a natural (as opposed to man-made) process. Therefore, human beings can do nothing to stop it.
- Global warming does not exist. It is a concept dreamed up by liberals to control people and the government.

The ideas listed above may not include all possible beliefs about global warming, but the list is sufficient to illustrate the power of the social construction of reality. As the different points should illustrate, depending on one's *belief,* a particular *reality* exists. Those beliefs are created through the process of meaning-making thought: Our emersion in a world of symbols that, depending on their use and prevalence, construct our understanding of the world, what matters, and what doesn't. It is these differing meanings, based in our cultural understandings and experiences, that create communication problems and conflicts.

Another example of how a simple construct can manifest in different meanings is the issue of status. Status does not exist in the world apart from humans; it is something that human beings have constructed to make meaning and differentiate and align themselves with certain others. Status is constructed differently depending on one's cultural values and beliefs. One example might be that of car ownership. In the United States, car ownership is commonly associated with status. However, depending on the region in which one lives and his or her socioeconomic bracket, "status" as communicated through car ownership might be expressed differently. In an affluent, upscale, and urban community, status might be communicated through the ownership of what is considered a luxury car, such as a Mercedes or BMW. In a community that is focused more on environmental values, the ownership of a Toyota Prius or other hybrid or electric car models might be seen as an expression of status. In a more rural or working class community, where more masculine values might hold sway, a big truck might be the symbol of success or status, such as ownership of a Ford F-250, while owning a Prius, would, in contrast, be seen as a sign of weakness or lack of membership in the community.

Beyond these differences in the actual manifestation or representation to others is the shared belief that car ownership denotes status in some way, or conversely, that it may negatively affect status. For example, few communities perceive an automobile in a functional way as a tool. This functional way would enable persons and communities to overlook the make, model, or cost of the vehicle when making purchase decisions and simply buy a car that gets the job done—transporting bodies and objects to work, school, or shopping venues. This alternate example of meaning showcases the power of symbols combined with values to construct our reality or how we view the world.

Once this understanding of reality is clear, it opens up an entirely different way of behaving and interpreting our world. It is this ability that is the focus of discursive leadership approaches. That is, with this understanding of reality, we can begin to view the manifestation of leadership as the use of symbols and behaviors to create organizational realities. The important element to consider is that others are part of that creation in that they filter symbols and behaviors through their own cultural and experiential lenses.

Opportunity to Reflect

How does the social construction of reality affect how you view leadership? How is your view of leadership based on your personal beliefs, experiences, and your membership in different groups, such as socioeconomic groups, professional organizations, political groups, etc.?

The Social Construction of Reality and Leadership

The social constructionist view of leadership enables us to see leadership differently in that it is not akin to a "substance" that resides in an individual. Instead, it is a process that emerges in a particular situation, a process that involves meaning making among the actors who are a part of that situation. "To wit, leadership is co-constructed, a product of sociohistorical and collective meaning-making, and negotiated on an ongoing basis through a complex interplay among leadership actors, be they designated or emergent leaders, managers, followers, or both."[6]

As the earlier discussion of management theories of leadership hopefully illustrated, an incontrovertible theory of leadership has been difficult to construct because of the tremendous amount of situational variability and subjective qualities of the phenomenon. Not everyone, for example, would agree that George W. Bush was an exemplar of leadership and the same might be said of Barack Obama. In other words, leadership is often in the eye of the beholder.

However, if we adapt a social constructionist view of reality, we can put aside our concern with approaches to leadership that attempt to pin down a universal set of attributes or behaviors that define the phenomenon and begin to recognize the importance of the contingent nature of reality. This contingency goes beyond situational leadership theories put forth by the management discipline in that it is based on the assumption that reality is radically contingent, that is, its emergence is highly dependent on the context of situations and the actors involved. This understanding of the radical contingency of reality preempts to a large degree any meaningful attempts to predict universal attributes or behaviors in terms of leadership and its manifestation.

To illustrate this concept of contingency, we can look at the work of Carroll and Gillen.[7] They urged researchers to consider the unsystematic ways in which management's classic functions—planning, organizing, coordinating, and controlling—may be achieved through unplanned, informal, and brief conversations. This work highlights the call by Henry Mintzberg to his colleagues to get rid of their constructs before collecting data, because they were essentially artificial in their rigor.

Carroll and Gillen's radically different approach to leadership might be seen as the precursor to the emergence of the field of discursive leadership, which is founded on the notion of the social construction of reality through communicative practice. This theory of leadership recognizes that the phenomenon is more inventive than analytical.[8] Rather than assuming that leadership exists in the individual, it recognizes that leadership is contested and emerges through the collective identities of the actors involved.

Without getting deeper into the theory, one of the most important results of a discursive understanding of leadership is that it is a process as noted. This notion is summed up by Sigman: "The process of communication itself...is consequential, and it is the 'nature' of that consequentiality that should...be the appropriate focus."[9] Thus, discursive approach focuses on how leadership is "brought off" through communication practices.

If thought of in this way, leaders become "practical actors," a notion that calls attention to the performative role of language in creating social realities.[10] Performative simply means that language is used to do things, that is, discursively construct what counts as the real world to the participants in that world.[11] Knights and Wilmott highlighted the contingent nature of leadership in calling it a "practical accomplishment" where social order might be experienced as routine and unproblematic but is really an uncertain, reflexive accomplishment.[12]

The implications of these views of leadership suggest that leaders must constantly enact their relationship to their followers.[13] They must repeatedly *perform* leadership through communicative practice. With this understanding of the performative nature of leadership, we can arrive at a revised definition of leadership: "Leadership is exercised when ideas expressed in talk or action are recognized by others as capable of progressing tasks or problems which are important to them."[14]

Table 1.3 Discursive versus psychological leadership approaches

Discursive leadership	Psychological leadership
Leadership outcomes determined by external factors	Utility of leadership from methods used by the individual
Primary interest in interpersonal communication	Primary interest in individual cognitive operation
Study leadership through analysis of interactions and outcomes	Study leadership using models and theories
Leader is effective because they correctly analyze context, de-center the subject, and adapt communication to meet goals within context	Leader is effective because of their traits and personality
Leadership is constructed in the moment through communication in context	Leadership is an analytical activity for the individual
Methods that work for one person may not work for another and what worked in one situation may not work in a similar situation	Leadership methods are prescriptive and work for everyone

An important difference in this approach to leadership as compared with management theories is that leadership is not an essence or attribute of an individual but is an attribution made by followers or observers.[15] A second important difference of this approach to leadership is communication becomes the primary concern rather than a secondary or tertiary consideration. Table 1.3 summarizes some of the distinctions between the discursive and psychological approaches to leadership.

The recognition of the importance of communication and of the performative nature of leadership is particularly of value to those aspiring to practice leadership or improve their leadership skills because it is potentially more empowering than the belief that leadership involves possessing a set of attributes or behaviors. It also provides for the possibility of having a clearer understanding of how leadership actually operates within organizational settings.

Opportunity to Reflect

How does the discursive theory of leadership differ from management perspectives of leadership? What does this mean in practical terms to actual or aspiring leaders?

Summary

Leadership is defined as the ability to influence a group toward the achievement of goals. The emphasis on influence helps us to better understand the differences between leadership and management. In other words, leaders often differ from managers in terms of the type of power they may yield. Managers are appointed; they have legitimate power or what is sometimes called "position power," which enables them to reward and punish employees. The formal authority given to them by their position within an organization gives managers the potential to influence employees. Leaders, on the other hand, may be appointed or may emerge. In the latter case, they have the opportunity to influence others beyond the formal authority assigned to them within an organization.

Broadly speaking, management theories have taken a psychological approach to leadership, which simply means that we assume the substance "leadership" is located within or an attribute of an individual. This psychological assumption about the basis of leadership as a kind of substance located within the individual has resulted in what may be viewed as four broad categories of leadership theory. These categories are trait, behavioral, contingency, and neocharismatic theories.

Trait theories assume that leaders demonstrate certain traits, such as charisma, enthusiasm, courage, honesty, self-confidence, and intelligence. The behavioral approach proposes that leadership is composed of two general kinds of behaviors: task and relationship behaviors. Task behaviors help group members achieve their objectives and goals, while relationship behaviors help subordinates feel valued and comfortable with each other and the situation. Similarly, situational leadership stresses that leadership is composed of two dimensions: directive and supportive. According to this theory, the leader should match his or her style to the competence and commitment of employees. Transformational leadership is the process whereby a person engages with others and creates a connection that raises moral and the level of motivation. This type of leader is attentive to the needs and motives of followers and tries to help followers reach their fullest potential.

The emergence of a discursive approach to leadership is in part due to what has been called the "linguistic turn." The linguistic turn considers that language is not used to make an accurate representation of reality if reality is defined as internal or external worlds that exist before our ability to use language. In other words, language is weighted in culture and thus carries values and meanings that reside in and are an outgrowth of culture. Our understanding of reality is thus already filtered through a lens laden with the values of our culture. Because of this, it is said that we cannot have an understanding of the world that exists without or before language.

The social constructionist view of leadership enables us to see leadership differently in that it is not akin to a "substance" that resides in an individual. Instead, it is a process that emerges in a particular situation, a process that involves meaning-making among the actors who are a part of that situation. Rather than assuming that leadership exists in the individual, it recognizes that leadership is contested and emerges through the collective identities of the actors involved. The implications of these views of leadership suggest that leaders must constantly enact their relationship to their followers. They must repeatedly *perform* leadership through communicative practice. An important difference in this approach to leadership as compared with management theories is that leadership is not an essence or attribute of an individual but is an attribution made by followers or observers. A second important difference of this approach to leadership is communication becomes the primary concern rather than a secondary or tertiary consideration.

CHAPTER 2

Introduction to the Elements of Leadership Talk

Max DePree popularized the idea that leadership is an art. So much of what a leader does cannot be objectively measured. To reduce leadership to a set of algorithms is to remove it from its context; to ignore the complexities, the contradictions, and the possibilities. Artists must deal with uncertainty, contradictions, and diversity almost by definition. Leaders need to have this capacity.

—Michael McKinney

In order to understand how to begin to see leadership as a product of communication practices or talk, you first need to develop the ability to pay attention to talk, to be able to identify the elements of talk, and then know and apply a framework(s) that allows you to assign greater fullness of meaning to what people say and how they say it. The next step is to develop an understanding of how the elements of talk are interpreted by others involved in the process of leadership emergence, since leadership is co-constructed by the participants in the interaction. This chapter will introduce ways of categorizing or identifying elements of talk with the intention of providing concrete examples of how leadership emerges in talk and an introductory framework for analyzing and understanding talk in action.

It is important to recognize that the concepts discussed here are drawn from broader disciplines, namely, linguistics and, to a lesser extent, communication. This discussion will thus attempt to address these elements without expectation of an extensive background in these academic disciplines. Therefore, those who do come to this discussion with that background and knowledge base in place may find that some of the issues relevant to their disciplines appear to be dealt with superficially or that some important elements are ignored or omitted. We ask that these omissions be forgiven with the thought that the intent of this discussion is to make some of the valuable contributions of these fields more accessible to practitioners.

For illustration purposes, the discussion presented here largely draws upon our own research in the area of group decision-making and leadership communication styles. Broadly speaking, this type of research is called *business discourse analysis* in which discourse refers to:

> talk and text in situational organizational contexts…[and] often examines the processes in which organizational actors [engage discourse to] construct emotion, attitude, identity and various aspects of organizational reality, accomplish work tasks and orderliness, and manage contradictions and work relationships through moment-to-moment talk-in-interaction and creation of local texts.[1]

As this definition implies, business discourse analysis is solidly grounded in a social constructionist perspective, which was discussed in Chapter 1.

Turn-Taking and Turn-Taking Strategies

An extensive background in linguistic theory and methods is not needed to understand the power of talk in action. For example, simple counting can provide useful insights into organizational interaction and leadership emergence. This type of approach is called *interaction analysis*, which is a quantitative approach to discourse analysis that draws from message functions and language structures, to assess the frequency and types of verbal interaction.[2]

The discussion that follows was drawn from several studies from which we identified six variables for tracking member interaction in a group decision-making situation.[3] To measure member contribution, we tracked the number of turns taken by participants, the number of words spoken, and the average turn length. We measured member participation by looking at turn-taking strategies. Turn-taking strategies include overlaps, backchannels, latching, and interruptions. These concepts are defined in the subsequent discussion.

Turn-Taking and Number of Words Spoken

As an introduction to the elements of discourse analysis, let's begin with the easily graspable notion of turn-taking. Turn-taking is a fundamental element of discourse analysis and can be defined as the ordering of moves that involves the interchange of talking by speakers.[4] Here's an illustration of turn-taking:

Susan:	Where shall we go for dinner tonight?
Juan:	How about that Thai place down on Fifth? We haven't been there for a while, and you know how much I love curry!

Turn-taking in combination with another simple dimension, number of words spoken, reveals additional insights about an interaction. To illustrate, we will use the results of a study we conducted that looked at how turn-taking and words spoken affected the quality of a group decision-making process involving participants from the United States and East Asian countries and conducted in English. Tables 2.1 and 2.2 summarize those results.

Table 2.1 provides the total number of turns taken, total number of words spoken, and average turn length for each team member in this particular group. Average turn length was derived by dividing the number of words spoken for each group member by his or her total turns taken. Taken together, these three variables were assumed to measure member contribution. As this table shows, the number of turns taken by those from East Asian cultures was significantly lower than those from the

Table 2.1 Contribution to decision-making meetings with a male group leader

Speaker	Total turns taken	Total words spoken	Average words per turn
S*1 U.S., Male	200	1962	9.81
S2 East Asian, Male	70	217	3.10
S3 U.S, Female	113	678	6.00
S4 U.S., Female	140	870	6.21
S5 East Asian, Male	8	38	4.75

* S stands for speaker as in Speaker 1.

Table 2.2 Contribution to decision-making meetings by cultural group

Total speakers	Average number of turns	Average number of words	Average words per turn
East Asian speakers	39	127.5	3.2
U.S. speakers	151	1170	7.7

Source: Aritz and Walker (2012).

United States and particularly the U.S. male. Similarly, the significance of this finding is dramatically illustrated if we compare the numbers of words spoken by the U.S. and East Asian participants who spoke the most words, 1,962 and 217, respectively.

This illustration shows how significant the simple act of counting turns taken and words spoken can be in terms of revealing the contribution of team members in a decision-making situation. That is, this act of counting illustrates that, in terms of collaboration, some members apparently are being significantly underutilized. From a leadership perspective, if we assume that the leader's role is at least in part to ensure that all members are contributing all of their potential knowledge and insights to the situation, these numbers also reveal potential problems regarding that role.

Table 2.2 brings this point home by illustrating the average number of turns taken and the average number of words spoken for each cultural group. On average, the American speakers took nearly four times the number of turns as their East Asian counterparts and contributed about nine times the number of words to the discussion. The average words per turn were more than twice as many for the American speakers than their East Asian counterparts. A third conclusion that thus might be drawn from this simple analysis is that in addition to leadership style, cultural differences and perhaps language proficiency potentially inhibited East Asian speakers' contribution rates. We will discuss the effect of culture in more detail in a later chapter, but for now this example illustrates how simple counting of turns taken and words spoken can reveal significant problems in terms of leadership and decision-making in a communication interaction such as a group discussion.

From a slightly different perspective, this example also reveals the power of talk to create reality in that talk in and of itself constituted this decision-making exchange—it was its "substance" to a large degree. In other words, this example provides an illustration of a subtle shift in focus away from the biological actor or person and to the way that words themselves not only reveal but also construct the content of the situation, that is, its substance or reality. This shift in focus, or *lens,* is required to grasp the power of talk in action. We can develop the ability to create and use different lenses through which we can interpret situations differently, depending on the lens that we apply. In this case, the lens is a discursive one; it requires the ability to focus on language, its use, and its effect.

Opportunity to Reflect

Using the last meeting that you participated in as an example, try to recall how often each member of the group spoke and how much each participant said and contributed to the discussion. If you participated in a meeting that included members from other cultural groups, reflect on the contribution rates of each. Were there any differences? What do think those differences represent? How did the leader address (if at all) or possibly contribute to the differences in the amount of talk each member contributed?

Turn-Taking Strategies: Overlaps, Interruptions, Backchannels, and Latching

Paying attention to other elements of talk can reveal additional characteristics of an interaction. As mentioned previously, in addition to looking at member contribution, we created a way to measure participation of group members by looking at turn-taking strategies. Turn-taking strategies include overlaps, interruptions, backchannels, and latching.

Conversational overlaps are defined as periods when both speakers talk at the same time and the conversational contribution of one speaker overlaps with that of another. If overlaps are cooperative, speakers do not change topic but elaborate upon the current one under discussion. Here's an example:

Speaker 1:	Creating a method of tracking information can [be done]
Speaker 2:	[tracking] information will enable us to notice if we need to adjust our schedule.

In this example, the brackets denote where the overlap in talk occurred. As this illustration shows, Speaker 1 introduced the topic of tracking information and Speaker 2 elaborates on this topic by overlapping Speaker 1's turn.

Overlaps can be viewed as what Deborah Tannen has called a high-involvement discourse style, which can be interpreted differently, depending on the perceiver.[5] For example, a positive interpretation of overlaps would see them as evidence of enthusiastic involvement and a collaborative approach to the discussion in which participants spontaneously build on one another's contribution. In contrast, a negative interpretation might consider overlaps as being fast-talking, pushy, or aggressive.

This contradictory interpretation of the same phenomenon illustrates another important aspect of the discursive approach, particularly as it applies to leadership emergence. That is, that the perception of what talk means is highly variable, depending on the person who is interpreting the talk. Because of this fact, what is seen as "leadership" may not be the same for all parties to an interaction.

Interruptions are another type of simultaneous speech and can be defined as instances where someone cuts in to talk about a different topic when the first speaker has not even made a single point.[6] Here's an example:

Jeanette:	I think we should begin by [introducing ourselves]
Frank:	[Tom, why don't you] take a quick head count to make sure we're all here?

In this example, Jeanette proposes that the meeting begin by members introducing themselves. Frank interrupts, proposing a different way of opening the meeting. It is implicit in this move that Frank does not agree with Jeanette's suggestion, since another idea is proposed. Furthermore, this proposition is made in such a way so as not to recognize Jeanette's suggestion. This lack of recognition of the other is generally considered impolite, or what might be called damaging to the "face" of the other, in this case, Jeanette. This assumption draws on Face Negotiation Theory, which assumes that embarrassing another can make some individuals uncomfortable, while avoiding embarrassing one's self is also a concern. In this example, potential embarrassment is caused by the lack of recognition of the "face" of the other person.

If viewed from a leadership perspective, another layer of meaning emerges from this encounter. That is, at the beginning of a meeting, Jeanette's proposition might be seen as an "offer" to be the leader. Frank's follow-up proposition can be seen as a simultaneous rejection of that offer and a counter-offer to be the leader. Group members will determine who comes out "on top" in that they must accept an offer of leadership; this notion will be more fully developed in the next section.

A third turn-taking strategy, **backchanneling**, gives the speaker an indication that the hearer is listening, paying attention, or both. Backchannels consist of such vocalizations as "yes," "uh huh," and "I see." "They are intended to keep the communication going by confirming or reacting to a preceding statement.[7] Some researchers regard backchanneling as a form of positive interruptions. Like other turn-taking strategies, backchanneling may have a more positive interpretation in that it can be seen as an affirmation of the other person, a form of recognition of what the other is saying. Consider the following actual exchange taken from a simulated exercise in which participants were asked to determine the items from a plane crash that would be necessary for survival purposes:

Speaker 1:	Oh, are you saying matches are more important than a compass?
Speaker 2:	Ya because you [need] heat. Whether you're [moving] or staying, still you're going to =
Speaker 1:	[Oh.] [Ya]
Speaker 2:	=need fire in [order to live].

If you notice, Speaker 1 is making minimal responses while Speaker 2 is speaking, "*oh*" and "*Ya.*" By doing so, S1 is encouraging S2 to continue and is validating S2's contribution. Research shows that women assign high value to listening and therefore tend to produce and expect backchannels as a sign of encouragement and validation. Men, on the other hand, often construct conversation as a competition and do not value listening as much. They also interpret backchannels as a sign of agreement rather than encouragement. As a result, the use or absence of backchannels leads to clashes in mixed gender interactions.

The fourth and final turn-taking strategy to be discussed is **latching**, which are instances in which a second speaker begins speaking without any perceptible pause but without overlapping with a previous speaker.[8] Here's an example:

Speaker 1:	What if we suggest to management that the forms are filled out first?z
Speaker 2:	zThat's a great suggestion. What do the rest of you think?

In the example, "z" indicates an instance of latching. Latching can be perceived as intrusive by some and not so by others. That is, latching can serve the function of active listenership and co-participation rather than being interpreted as a type of interruption. Often this difference in perception or interpretation, along with those identified earlier, are attributable to cultural differences. (The effect of culture on the interpretation of discourse and its elements will be addressed in more detail in Chapter 6. Gender as another cultural construct that can affect the interpretation of meaning will be addressed in Chapter 5.)

As this discussion is intended to illustrate, turn-taking strategies can enable participation among those involved in an interaction or cut it off. Depending on the person interpreting the use of each strategy, turn-taking can be perceived as having a negative or positive effect on the productiveness of the conversation. Some turn-taking strategies, depending on the time of their occurrence, the content, and the phrasing, can also be seen as propositions to serve as the leader. In the next section, the issue of phrasing will be discussed in greater detail to show its potential impact on interactions.

Opportunity to Reflect

Using the last meeting that you participated in as an example, try to recall the turn-taking strategies used by participants as well as by yourself. What was the effect of those turn-taking strategies on the quality of participation of those involved in the discussion? Are there turn-taking strategies that you tend to favor? Based on this discussion, how might those contribute to or detract from the participation rates of those with whom you interact? How might these strategies be interpreted by others? What changes might you make in your turn-taking strategy use, if any, to enhance your perception as a leader by those with whom you commonly interact?

Illocutionary Force: Use of Questions and Aggression

Since leadership is an attempt to influence others, it is important to consider the intention of the speaker when we look at leadership talk. The speaker's intention is called *illocutionary force*. Different intentions of talk include promising, advising, warning, asserting, inquiring, and ordering.

An example of illocutionary force is the query, "How's that soup coming? Is it ready yet?" as a way of (politely) inquiring about the status of the soup in the context of ordering food at a restaurant. The actual intent of the statement may be, in fact, to <u>make the waiter bring the soup</u>. In other words, the illocutionary force of the statement is not an inquiry about the progress of soup preparation, but a <u>demand</u> that the soup be brought.

Illocutionary force will be explored in this section by looking at the use of questions. Questions illustrate the variety of meanings that can emerge from a simple sentence structure that most of us take for granted. Questions are a form of speech that typically require or intend a response. Because of this expectation, they can ensure that conversation continues. Earlier research posited that questions have two purposes; they may be direct in purpose, that is, they may be simply asking a question, or they may be used indirectly to facilitate discussion.[9] Here is an example of a question that is direct in purpose:

Friend: Do you want to catch a movie?

This question is direct in that the speaker is simply asking for agreement or disagreement. It can be answered with a simple "Yes" or a "No."

In the example below, the question is indirectly used for the second purpose, to facilitate discussion:

Manager: Lois, what are your thoughts on the proposal?

Questions can also be used for a third purpose (depending upon how they are phrased and the context of the discussion) to direct agreement. Here's an example:

Manager: I think that option 1 is the best solution, wouldn't you all agree?

The *context* of the situation, or setting, can add a good deal to the interpretation of this question. As mentioned in Chapter 1, the manager has position power within an organization. As such, in this example, disagreeing with the speaker (who is the manager) may, depending on his or her style of communication and the culture of the organization, involve a risk to the employee. In other words, the manager's use of language over time may tend to be directive rather than inclusive or collaborative when communicating with employees. This history, which creates part of the context of the discussion, may lead employees to interpret the question as more of a directive—"You do agree with me"—than as a question that warrants a response that may involve disagreement.

Similarly, the question would not be considered an invitation to suggest new ideas, if the context indicated that it was not being used to solicit this sort of reply. The illocutionary act, the question, may thus have different intentions, depending on the speaker and the context in which he or she is operating.

Questions can also be used more aggressively as this example shows:

Discussion participant: <u>Who</u> thought of <u>that</u>?

Aggression can be indicated by tone of voice and sentence structure. In this example, the vocal emphasis on the words "who" and "that" create a negative tone that implies that the idea referred to by "that" is not a good one and thus that the offerer of the idea was not thinking well. As this example shows, the combination of tone of voice—derisive—and sentence structure—a question, indicates a negative judgment about the person whose name is the answer to the question as well as that person's statement.

Sometimes aggression is implicit in that it emerges from the inferential nature of the statement. In the following example taken from the plane crash simulated exercise, Speaker 1 is arguing for the item "matches":

Speaker 1:	I figure you can use fire; otherwise, you're screwed.
Speaker 4:	Okay, so let's
Speaker 3:	z but if you, but if you just have matches what are you going to do with [them?]

The use of the question, "what are you going to do with them?" must be interpreted in combination with the phrase, "if you just have matches." Combined, this question could be interpreted to mean "what are you going to do with matches if you don't have any fuel?" This interpretation can be seen as somewhat aggressive, since it implicitly points out the illogic of arguing for matches. In other words, it could be intended or interpreted as saying Speaker 1's position is illogical or misguided. This inference could be considered aggressive in that it is implying a negative judgment about Speaker 1. The use of the question, though, is strategic in that it serves as an indirect criticism rather than a direct statement regarding the quality of the idea. This can be illustrated by stating the idea a bit more directly, "Matches are useless if you don't have fuel," or even more directly with "That's not a good idea. If you don't have fuel, matches are useless." This final assertion could be seen as even more aggressive because it states a fact, rather than questions the situation. The question has a softening effect that the assertion does not.

As with the use of questions, aggression may also emerge from the context or from the situation. An illustration in the earlier example is reproduced below:

| Jeanette: | I think we should begin by [introducing ourselves] |
| Frank: | [Tom, why don't you] take a quick head count to make sure we're all here? |

The context is the beginning of a meeting. From that context, we might interpret Frank's question as carrying several meanings. First, it proposes a different start to the meeting—taking a head count—than that suggested by Jeanette, and as such, it might also be considered as an offer or proposition to take on the role of leader. Even though phrased as a question, it is not expecting a "yes" or "no" response; it carries the illocutionary force of a directive. Because it is an interruption that proposes an alternate start to the meeting, it can be considered aggressive because there is no recognition of Jeanette's previous proposition.

Other sentence structures as well as word choices can communicate aggressiveness, as shown in the following examples:

- "Shut up!" (a directive)
- "That's a dumb suggestion." (an assertion)
- "You should all see the only reasonable decision."(an assertion)
- "Anyone can see what needs to be done." (an assertion)
- Close the door! (a directive)

These speech acts are of interest in that unlike a question that is part of the conversational sequence Question and Answer, they do not necessarily require a response. This issue will be discussed in more detail in the next section.

Opportunity to Reflect

Have you considered how the simple speech form of a question might be used to indicate various intentions? How do you commonly use questions in office interactions? Could their use be considered aggressive by others? How might you become more aware of how the sentence forms you use reinforce your actual intentions or how these sentence forms may be interpreted differently by others than your intent?

Sequential Properties of Talk and Identity Creation

In the 1960s, Harvey Sacks and his colleagues developed a method for analyzing the structure of talk-in-interaction in order to arrive at an "enormous understanding of the way humans do things and the kind of objects they use to construct order in their affairs."[10] This method is called *conversation analysis*. In 1986, Sacks further developed this method by pioneering the idea of examining the link between the sequential properties of talk and the identities of the participants.[11] Using this method, identities are seen as "membership categories." That is, identities are "talked into being" through orientation to the sequences of talk.[12] A classroom can illustrate this concept if seen as a communicative event typified or constructed by the initiation-response-feedback sequence of interaction:

> Teacher and student identities are "talked into being" through orientation to these sequences of talk. Initiating interaction in the first turn and evaluating that interaction in a third turn makes participation orientation to "teacher" identity relevant and responding in a second turn makes "student" identity relevant.[13]

In other words, in a classroom situation, we have been taught that the "teacher" initiates discussion, while the "student" responds. The response is generally followed by "teacher" feedback. In this context-sensitive interaction, we have been taught to follow specific rules; perhaps more importantly, the rules also define the roles of the participants.

This is one of the cornerstones of conversation analysis: The assumption that talk is sequentially ordered in adjacent pairs that are produced by different speakers. That is, talk is ordered as a first part and a second part and designed so that a particular first requires a particular second.[14] This idea was introduced earlier in the discussion of the question as a particular speech form. A question would be considered the first part of an adjacency pair while a response would be the second part.

Another example of adjacency pairs is an invitation. Invitations are required to be accepted or rejected and if neither response occurs in a second turn, they are "oriented to as being noticeably absent."[15] Thus, there are preferences for certain second-pair parts, and the absence of the second pair has meaning, or is "marked."

To illustrate this point, let's look at another example taken from the plane crash simulation exercise. In this situation, the participants are discussing whether a compass would be a useful item.

Speaker 4:	z I've been in lots of woods, I mean I've been in the woods before it's, it's hard. Without some so[rt of] guidance
Speaker 2:	[like] z mhmm
Speaker 5:	well uh,
Speaker 1:	z what did you guys put as the number one?

In this example, Speaker 4 attempts to show that he has relevant expertise needed to make the decision about the compass by stating that he has been in the woods and knows from that experience that it can be difficult to navigate without some kind of guidance, that is, a compass. In other words, Speaker 4's move could be seen as an attempt to categorize himself as "an expert" in this particular situation. What we see in the responses of speakers 2, 5, and 1 that follow, however, are "a noticeable absence" in that the expected response—to affirm Speaker 4's claim—does not materialize. What this means is that Speaker 4's attempt to categorize himself as an expert was not accepted by the other members, that is, that identity did not emerge or become concrete in this interaction.

This example, like the classroom exchange, illustrates how particular identities are created in interaction with others—they do not necessarily reside as a characteristic within the individual. This understanding is important for those who aspire to be seen as a leader. Such a person needs to understand that within a particular culture or group, certain categories exist that are related to certain roles or identities. Thus, to be seen as having a particular identity, the person must project the characteristics of that identity, of following the conversational rules associated with that role or both. Even if this is accomplished through conscious intention, though, it does not mean that the action will be successful if the other participants do not see or accept the individual as fitting the particular category or they do not "know" or "obey" the rules associated with a particular context.

The process of negotiating an identity involves three sequential tasks: "invoking social identities, negotiating what the features or boundaries of those identities are, and accumulating a record of having those identities."[16]

In other words, individuals must present themselves as having certain characteristics associated with a particular identity, follow the rules associated with that particular role, and over time and through interactions with others, draw on these past impressions to accrue a particular identity within that particular context. By extension, then, identities are flexibly defined in the moment but are also seen as relatively stable to the degree that the individuals consistently orient to particular features or boundaries of a particular role across interactions with others.[17] It is through this process that the identity of "leader" emerges over time.

Opportunity to Reflect

Have you considered how the interaction rules in your workplace construct certain relationships among members? If so, what are the sequences that are commonly used and how do they help to "place" communicators in certain roles? In those interactions, what does your sequence in these conversations say about your role in the organization?

Framing

The word "framing" has many connotations; however, in this discussion it is used to mean framing a situation in terms of its meaning, or more simply, "framing reality." The strategy of framing is commonly used in political discourse. Such statements as "we're on the road to prosperity," for example, are an attempt by the speaker to frame the current reality as one in which the economy is improving dramatically. To the extent that the speaker can follow up on that claim with some convincing anecdotes or what appears to the listener to be adequate evidence, he or she may be successful in creating that reality or belief in the listener. The "truth" may in fact be quite different: the majority of economic indicators may show that the economy is making little or no improvement. But by using stories that evoke a positive emotional response from the listener and by "cherry picking" some positive facts from the economic indicators, the speaker may be successful in creating a positive picture for the listener, one that he or she believes or is convinced is true. In the latter case, the speaker has created reality for the listener through his or her word choice and arrangement. That creation, though, is only successful if the listener agrees to or accepts the reality that is offered by the speaker.

Framing can also be used in an organizational setting to create certain "realities." A frame can be as simple as defining a situation in black-and-white terms, or what is called an either/or situation: "We have only two choices: Close the plant or lay off workers!" If the audience accepts a frame as the reality, then the frame was successful, regardless of whether it is in fact "true." This is another example of the creation of social reality at work; in other words, what we agree is reality, is reality, regardless of its factual basis.

Conversely, though, the audience might also respond, "That is not true. There are many other options. We can (1) look for lower-cost suppliers, (2) reduce wages for all employees, (3) reduce wages for some employees, (4) eliminate unproductive product lines, (5) subcontract some of our services to reduce fixed costs, (6) flatten our hierarchy and reassign high-salary individuals" and so on. In this latter case, the frame was not successful, since it was not accepted by the listener. The listener, in fact, offered other "realities."

In a workplace context, framing can be very useful for leaders in terms of defining situations so that people are more likely to be motivated or even inspired by a certain reality. "Today marks the beginning of a new era for ABC Technology with the introduction of our next-generation product line." Such a statement draws upon words and phrases commonly used in political discourse to evoke positive images and emotions associated with the future: "marks the beginning," "new era," "introduction," and "next generation." Again, depending on the credibility of the speaker, the history of use of such discourse in the organization, its veracity, the current state of the economy, the current financial condition of the company, the current morale of employees, and so forth—in other words, the context—this frame may or may not be successful.

As was discussed in the previous section, a person also might attempt to frame himself or herself as a leader. For example, framing one's self as an expert can sometimes help one to gain the ability to influence. As discussed in Chapter 1, *expert power* is defined as influence based on the target's belief that the power holder possesses superior skills and abilities.[18] From this definition, it should be clear that whether a person "is" an expert or not is to some degree inconsequential; what matters is that the target *believes* that the power holder possesses superior skills and abilities.

To illustrate this point, let's look again at the example used in the previous section which included an actual exchange from the plane crash simulated exercise. In this example, participants are discussing whether a compass would be a necessary item for survival:

Speaker 4:	z I've been in lots of woods, I mean I've been in the woods before it's, it's hard. Without some so[rt of] guidance
Speaker 2:	[like] z mhmm
Speaker 5:	well uh,
Speaker 1:	z what did you guys put as the number one?

As discussed earlier, Speaker 4 attempts to show that he has relevant expertise needed to make the decision about the compass by stating that he has been in the woods and that, based on that experience, it can be difficult to navigate without some kind of guidance, that is, a compass. As the example illustrates, even though Speaker 4 attempted to frame himself as an expert in this limited area of knowledge, his attempt didn't gain much traction. Speakers 2 and 5 appear not to know how to respond to his frame or are reluctant to give it weight as evidenced by the use of disfluencies or what are commonly called "fillers" ("mhmm" and "well, uh") used to fill uncomfortable silences. Speaker 1 then attempts to move the discussion forward by again asking the question that initiated the exchange. In other words, Speaker 1 changes the topic and reorients the discussion. This exchange shows how silence (as expressed through disfluencies, in this case) can be read as a form of polite disagreement, as direct disagreement is not expressed. The silence is thus used to save face with respect to Speaker 4.

What we don't have access to are the thoughts of the other participants to know why Speaker 4's attempt to frame himself as an expert didn't receive an affirmative response. Still, this example shows that expertise, which we often assume resides in the individual as a characteristic, can also be viewed as a proposition that can either be accepted or denied by others.

Within an organizational setting, the characteristic "expertise" might be evoked many times by an individual through various communication practices, including those involving the body (i.e., "body language"). The result may be that the characteristic "expertise" as it has been given to us through our cultural beliefs and values begins to adhere to that individual. Once this has occurred, it can then evolve to be seen as a characteristic that resides in him or her. This is the key difference between management and discursive approaches to leadership; many management theories of leadership are based on the assumption that the characteristics associated with leadership reside within the individual. In contrast, discursive leadership argues that they are perceptions created and negotiated through a series of social interactions.

Becoming or establishing oneself as a leader can be viewed as the process of the social construction of reality at work in that we have cultural categories or roles created through social interaction before our time and delivered to us *in situ*. A person with knowledge of these cultural categories can thus reproduce the behaviors associated with a particular type or role to be then seen as "being" of that type, in this case an "expert." This process of framing our communication so that we are seen as being of a particular cultural type can be achieved through conscious or intuitive choice by the individual. The conscious choice involves what is called "strategic thinking," which also requires an awareness of the cultural categories and roles that need to be reproduced to achieve particular ends and the conversational techniques that bring those roles into being. This chapter has introduced some foundational concepts to begin thinking about the latter issue, but this discussion only skims the surface of methods or frameworks that can be applied to interpret talk in action. The next chapter will discuss how particular leadership styles emerge in interaction with others and their effect on that interaction.

Opportunity to Reflect

Identify situations in your organization in which different individuals have attempted to frame reality. Was the frame successful or not? Why? What opportunities exist for you to frame reality in your workplace? What competing "realities" exist that may stand in your way of doing so? Might those competing realities be altered over time? If so, how and by whom?

Summary

This chapter provided readers with a way to think about language use and how it can create social realities. It also introduced elements of language that can be used to construct social realities though language.

The first of these elements, turn-taking strategies, include overlaps, backchannels, latching, and interruptions.

- Turn-taking is a fundamental element of discourse analysis and can be defined as the ordering of moves that involves the interchange of talking by speakers.
- Conversational overlaps are defined as periods when both speakers talk at the same time and the conversational contribution of one speaker overlaps with that of another. If overlaps are cooperative, speakers do not change topic but elaborate upon the current one under discussion.
- Interruptions are another type of simultaneous speech and can be defined as instances where someone cuts in to talk about a different topic when the first speaker has not even made a single point.
- Backchanneling gives the speaker an indication that the hearer is listening, paying attention, or both. Backchannels consist of such vocalizations as "yes," "uh huh," and "I see." They are intended to keep the communication going by confirming or reacting to a preceding statement.
- Latching refers to instances in which a second speaker begins speaking without any perceptible pause but without overlapping with a previous speaker.

Since leadership is an attempt to influence others, it also is important to consider the intention of the speaker when we look at leadership talk. The speaker's intention is called illocutionary force. Different intentions of talk include promising, advising, warning, asserting, inquiring, and ordering. Illocutionary force can be fruitfully explored by looking at the variety of ways that questions might be used in interactions. Questions are often used to ensure that conversation continues, to simply ask a question, and to facilitate discussion. They can also be used more aggressively to direct agreement or as indirect criticism, among other things.

Another way to think about talk is to look at its sequential nature. This is based on the assumption that talk is sequentially ordered in adjacent pairs that are produced by different speakers. That is, talk is ordered as a first part and a second part and designed so that a particular first requires a particular second. This idea is illustrated by the use of a question as a particular speech form that requires a response. The process of negotiating an identity can also be seen as a sequential task in that it involves invoking an identity, negotiating its features or boundaries, and accumulating a record of having those features. In other words, individuals must present themselves as having certain characteristics associated with a particular identity, follow the rules associated with that particular role, and over time and through interactions with other individuals, draw on these past impressions to accrue a particular identity within that particular context.

Framing a situation means to identify or define its outline or structure. Framing can thus be used in an organizational setting to create certain "realities." Similarly, a person also might attempt to frame himself or herself as a leader by, for example, claiming expertise.

CHAPTER 3

Leadership Communication Styles

I suppose leadership at one time meant muscles; but today it means getting along with people.

—Mahatma Gandhi

As discussed in Chapter 1, the trajectory of development of traditional models of leadership has enabled us to recognize that a "one-size-fits-all" approach to leadership doesn't always work. That is, the basic assumption of behavioral and contingency or situational theories of leadership is that the leader must adapt his or her style to the demands of the situation. As was discussed in Chapter 1, situational leadership theory stresses that leadership is composed of two dimensions—directive and supportive—that build on the assumptions developed by the earlier behavioral theorists. According to situational leadership theory, leaders should change the degree to which they are directive or supportive, depending on the shifting needs of employees, the situation, or both. These theories suggest that the leader should match his or her style to the competence and commitment of employees. For example, if a leader is working with a group with a low skill level, he or she might need to be more directive. If the group is highly skilled and motivated, the leader may not need to provide a great deal of direction but instead should focus on creating an environment where employees feel valued and recognized for their contribution.

One of the problems with the situational leadership approach is the inability to directly correlate employee behavior to those of the leader. In other words, this approach doesn't acknowledge the challenge that is presented by understanding that the phenomenon "leadership" is constructed and emerges from the interaction of followers and the person who presumes to be the leader; it is a co-construction of all of the participants to the interaction. This approach—with its focus on the leader—also does not explicitly acknowledge the effects of leadership style on the participants and the overall quality of the interaction.

This chapter will illustrate how three styles of leadership emerge from the talk involved in group interactions: the directive, the cooperative, and the collaborative styles. These styles were identified in a study that involved observations of 20 teams of business professionals involved in decision-making meetings.[1] The three leadership styles discussed here exemplify the most common of the successful leadership attempts that emerged from these observations. The discussion will show how each style emerges: In Chapter 6, this discussion will be continued to show how each style affects the participation and contribution of group members with a look at cultural differences. The chapter will close with a discussion of a confounding factor that we have observed in our research—the perception of expertise, a phenomenon that was introduced in Chapter 2.

Method for Analyzing and Identifying Leadership Communication Styles

The meetings that were the basis of this assessment involved a simulation called Subarctic Survival, which asked each group to take the role of airplane crash survivors. Groups were then asked to discuss and ultimately agree upon the ranking of items salvaged from the aircraft in terms of their critical function for survival.

The meetings were videotaped, transcribed, and then analyzed using the conversation analysis (CA) approach developed by Sacks.[2] As discussed in the previous chapter, the basic premise of CA is that by analyzing the structure of talk-in-interaction, the researcher can arrive at an understanding of how people do things, accomplish their goals, and construct order in their actions "by spelling out the communicative conventions and rules of various management activities."[3] Studies in conversation analysis show that turn-taking serves as the mechanism for decision-making that involves organized sequences of interaction exchange.

Our specific method of analysis of turn-taking is based on a model developed by Coates to analyze naturally occurring interactions in which she describes cooperative and competitive conversational styles.[4] Her method was selected to give us additional tools to provide a finer grained analysis of our data. Coates' model focuses on the following areas: (1) the meaning of questions—are they direct in purpose or used indirectly to facilitate conversation? (2) links between speaker turns—does the speaker acknowledge the contribution of the previous speaker or talk on the topic without acknowledging that contribution? (3) topic shifts—are they abrupt or do speakers build on each other's contributions? (4) listening—is the speaker using backchannels or latching? and (5) simultaneous speech—do the speakers overlap by elaborating on the previous contribution or does the contribution of the second speaker contradict or disrupt that of the first speaker? (All of these elements were explained in greater detail in Chapter 2.)

These interactional elements were used to analyze how their combination affects the emergence of leadership within teams of business professionals. This assessment did not include nonverbal clues, such as gaze and gestures, because our focus was on language and the unit of analysis was limited to a turn as a vehicle to construct leadership in talk.

The Directive Leadership Communication Style

In the following discussion, excerpts from a transcript of a group decision-making meeting will be used to show the emergence of the directive leadership style based upon the use of the previously discussed elements.

In the transcript excerpts, "S" refers to Speaker and is paired with a number to differentiate each of the participants in the discussion. Each line of the discussion is also numbered for easy identification. "z" refers to latching, while "xxxx" indicates words that were inaudible, likely due to an overlap, which is indicated by words or words enclosed in brackets, for example [...]..

In our discussion we will focus on Speaker 1 (S1) in all transcripts since S1 designates the leader in each group.

Use of Questions

Lines 1–35 of the transcript show Speaker 1 (S1) emerging as a group leader. In line 1, S1 is the first to announce his choice of the most vital item for survival, matches: "I figure you can use fire, otherwise you're screwed." In what follows, S1 uses questions in a competitive way to defend his decision. When his choice of the most important item for survival gets questioned in line 3, he interrupts S4 in line 6 and uses a tag question to challenge an alternative choice, "[well] at least you can start a fire, though, don't you think?"

1.	S1: I figure you can use fire, otherwise you're screwed.
2.	S4: Okay, so let's
3.	S3: z but if you, but if you just have matches what are you going to do
4.	with [them?]
5.	S4: [Yea] at least with the [xxxx]
6.	S1: [well] at least you can start a fire though, don't you think?
7.	… I mean it could be one or two, it doesn't matter

In line 22 of the transcript, S1 uses an indirect question to reassert his point, "You know what I am saying?" In line 31, S1 asserts himself again and has his first choice of matches recorded as the group decision. Speaker 1 does not use questioning as a way to facilitate conversation or solicit information from other team members but instead uses questions to direct them to select his preferred option.

Interestingly, the only team members questioning S1's choice are other native speakers of English. For example, in line 3, S3 makes an attempt to question the choice of matches as the number 1 item: "but if you, but if you just have matches, what are you going to do with them?" When S4 offers an alternative ranking in line 16, "Okay, so, are we doing sleeping bag first and the matches second?" She is not successful at introducing an alternative ranking as S1 takes the group back to his number one choice in line 17 by saying, "um… I think that just not having fire is like…"

Links Between Speaker Turns

Speaker 1 does not link with the previous speaker's contribution but rather concentrates on making his own point as shown in the excerpt below. The only acknowledgements of others that Speaker 1 makes is when the previous speaker supports S1's point, as illustrated below:

19.	S3: [That's true because] it's light and
20.	[it's heat]
21.	S1: [it's suicide] z Yea, it's light and its heat and 'cuz either way if you start a fire, the warmth is better than any sleeping bag. You know what I'm saying?

Topic Shifts

Speaker 1 does not attempt to create smooth transitions between topics. In line 16, S4 asks a question that invites a discussion; however, in line 17, S1 shifts the topic back to his agenda and forgoes the possibility to open the discussion to consider additional items, "um...XXX I think that just not having fire is like..."

16.	S4: Okay, so, are we doing sleeping bag first and the matches second? Or the other way around?
17.	S1: um...XXX I think that just not having fire is like [XXXX]

There is little elaboration and continuity of the topics introduced into the conversation; instead, Speaker 1 shifts abruptly to his agenda, to record matches as the most important item for the groups' survival.

Verbal Aggressiveness

The tone of voice and intonation manifested by loud talk and a fast pace express a high involvement conversation style as used by S1. In addition, S1 uses questions as indirect speech acts to express a directive.

Listening

Speaker 1 does not use minimal responses in the form of "yeah" and "mhm" to signal listening. In this case, the gender of the speaker might be an issue, because it has been found that for men, minimal responses signal agreement rather than listening and support as they do for women.[5] Their main conversational strategy—to seize the turn—places little value on listening and thus minimal responses rarely occur in their speech. (The issue of gender will be discussed more in Chapter 5.)

Simultaneous Speech

Speaker 1 uses overlaps that interrupt the previous speaker numerous times rather than cooperative overlaps that support the previous speaker's contribution, as seen in line 6 in the previous dialog box, and lines 21, 23, and 26 in the following dialog box. This, again, may be an issue of gender, since it has been shown that male speakers value speakership and therefore grab the floor by interrupting and violating the current speaker's right to complete the turn. In addition, men then tend to respond to interruptions by continuing to speak and keeping the floor, as Speaker 1 does in line 21.

21.	S1:	[it's suicide] z Yea, it's light and it's heat and 'cuz either way if you start a fire, the warmth is better than any sleeping bag. You know what I'm saying?
23.	S3:	Th[at's true, that's true.]
24.		[you can also xxxxxx]
25.	S2:	[xxx]
26.	S4:	[es]pecially if you find shelter and it's going to rain
27.	S1:	and if z and you [and] you're wet

Speaker 2 latches once, validating Speaker 1's "Okay," and tries to take the floor unsuccessfully twice. He and Speaker 5 are relatively silent.

This discussion illustrates the way that the elements of Coates' model are used to identify the constituent parts of a directive style of leadership. To summarize, a directive leader uses questions to direct agreement upon interaction participants, doesn't link his or her comments to the previous speaker's statement, makes abrupt topic shifts, uses minimal active listening techniques, tends to be verbally aggressive, and interrupts other speakers.

Opportunity to Reflect

Do you or someone you know typically use the Directive Leadership style? If this is your preferred style, are there some benefits to learning different leadership styles? If the Directive Leadership style applies to someone you know, what are its benefits? Its disadvantages? Does it match the culture of your organization? Why or why not?

The Cooperative Leadership Communication Style

The following discussion is from a transcript of a group-decision making meeting in which a more cooperative style of leadership emerges.

Use of Questions

At the beginning of this meeting, it looks as if Speaker 6 may take the leadership role. In line 2 of the discussion, he opens the discussion by asking,

"Okay, which of you chose, the uh, most important one?" S6 is quite active in the initial stage of the discussion taking three significant turns.

It is through the use of questions, though, that Speaker 1 emerges as a group leader a couple of minutes into the discussion. Instead of using questions to assert her own position or challenge others as a Directive Leader might, Speaker 1 asks closed and open-ended questions to solicit information about other group members' choices, "Did everyone choose the compass?" In line 36, she directs the question to two Asian females who have not yet spoken, giving them a chance to join the group, "What did you guys put as the number one?" Later in the meeting, she recaps the group discussion by summarizing and listing the items in order, "I think that, I think that the compass is good and then should we do the canvas as second?" which elicits an affirmative confirmation by other speakers. By then this more inclusive style as compared with the Directive Leader establishes Speaker 1 as the leader in this case. She takes on a more vocal leadership role in the remainder of the transcript.

Links Between Speaker Turns

In contrast to the Directive Leader who did not link his comments to those of the previous speaker, Speaker 1 acknowledges the contribution of the previous speaker on several occasions. In line 46, for example, she acknowledges S6's contribution and elaborates on the topic that he introduced, "oh really? To stay warm." Similarly, in lines 62 and 65, she continues on a topic that had been previously introduced by latching and overlapping with S5:

61.	S5: Have you ever stayed in the middle of snow? You have no idea where you are.
62.	S1: z you don't
63.	even know w[hat's] up or down.
64.	S5: [with] z pu[re snow, complete snow] you have no
65.	S1: [everything looks the same]

Topic Shifts

Speaker 1 uses elaboration and continuity as opposed to the sudden topic shifts demonstrated by the Directive Leader. Even when she changes the topic in line 73, her talk is linked to the previous speaker's contribution, creating a smooth transition that guides the team in its discussion:

72.	S5:	z I'm I'm I'm just saying that we agree on [the com]pass
73.	S1:	[yeahhhh] z I think that, I think
74.		that the compass is good and then [should we do the canvass] as second?

Listening

Although Speaker 1 uses just a few minimal responses, her participation is marked by active listening techniques. She actively participates in the conversation by using repetition (line 41) and by validating and elaborating on the previous speaker's turn (line 46):

36.	S1:	*z what did you guys put*
37.		*as the number one?*
38.	S4:	z what'd you get?
39.	S3:	z I put, I put canvass [not xxxxx]
40.	S5:	[oh canvass] is uh tent, the tent
41.	S1:	*z oh*
42.		*canvass*
43.	S4:	z oh canvass
44.	S6:	uh canvass, I put sleeping bag
45.	S5:	z ye[ah]
46.	S1:	*[oh really? To stay warm.]*

She also uses frequent latching and speaks without waiting for a pause in a way that validates and supports the previous speaker's contribution (lines 41 and 46).

Simultaneous Speech

Speaker 1 overlaps rarely, and when she does, her overlaps are cooperative, as shown in lines 46 and 65 in the previous examples. She does not use simultaneous speech to interrupt a previous speaker as was the case with the Directive Leader. On one occasion, she uses backchanneling— "yeahhh"—to show solidarity with S5.

This discussion illustrates the way that the elements of Coates' model are used to identify the constituent parts of a cooperative style of leadership. To summarize, a cooperative leader uses questions to solicit information or participation from others, acknowledges the position or statement of previous speakers, avoids abrupt topic shifts, uses active listening techniques, and uses cooperative overlaps to show her support of other's ideas.

Opportunity to Reflect

Do you or someone you know typically use the Cooperative Leadership style? If this is your preferred style, are there some benefits to learning different leadership styles? If the Cooperative Leadership style applies to someone you know, what are its benefits? Its disadvantages? Does it match the culture of your organization? Why or why not?

The Collaborative Leadership Communication Style

The following discussion is from a transcript of a group-decision making meeting in which a collaborative style of leadership emerges.

Use of Questions

In this group, the questions in the very beginning are used to establish the collaborative nature of interaction in the group. The first couple of questions as shown in lines 10 and 11 in the following dialog box are used by several members of the group to frame the type of discussion that will follow. The questions frame the type of discussion as collaborative as all the team members are more actively engaged in co-constructing the rules and the process for discussion.

10. S2: Do we wanna go around and just give like [our top 5?]	
11. S1: [What's the best?], what's the [least]=	
12. S5: [Sure.]	

Links Between Turns

Because of the collaborative nature of this group, the recognition of previous contributions is minimal but is present and positive. This can be seen in the "Okay" in line 90 and the "Ya" of agreement by Speaker 4 in lines 87 and 93 in this example:

87.	S4: [Ya, and I] figure if you can't drink the streams, you can use the mirror to help.
88.	you melt the water and then [you] just drink the snow.
89.	S2: [Or]
90.	S1: Okay.
91.	S2: Or I was gonna say, you can, you can melt the snow in the metal can [from the
92.	matches =
93.	S4: [Ya, that's

Topic Shifts

Speakers in this group tended to acknowledge and build on the previous speaker's contribution and topic shifts were not abrupt but were instead, constructive. For example, in the previous example, in line 91, Speaker 2 elaborates on Speaker 1's idea and proposes a variation that is introduced as an option by using a connector "or" that does not sound like an abrupt topic shift but more like a productive exploration of different alternatives.

Listening

The collaborative nature of the meeting can be seen in the use of multiple backchannels that signal listening and agreement. Speaker 3 and Speaker 2 use minimal positive acknowledgements of others' contribution in the form of "Ya" in lines 110 and 113. S2 and S5 signal their agreement by using minimal responses, "true" in line 118 and then "right" in line 120. Lines 122 and 124 show multiple minimal responses, "right right" and then "okay," that support the previous speaker and validate that the group is moving in the preferred direction in their decision-making process.

108.	S5: Well I put [as] my, my highest, uh the umm, the matches cause like you're, you're
109.	wet =
110.	S3: [Ya].
111.	S5: = [to the] waist, you're heavily perspiring. You're going to freeze to death
112.	because it's =
113.	S2: [Ya.]

114.   S5: = it's almost certainly below freezing at that point and so you need to first,
115.   before anything else get warm and dry.
116.   S1: I had [that,] I had that originally as matches. Actually I had, uh, matches and
117.   Bacardi =
118.   S2:   [True].
119.   S1: = because you can use Bacardi as fuel.
120.   S5: Right.
121.   S1: As lighter fluid.
122.   S5: Right. Right.
123.   S2: Okay.

Simultaneous Speech

In this group, there are frequent overlaps, but they are cooperative in the sense that they build or expand on, or productively question the previous speaker's contribution. For example, S4 and S5 overlap in lines 281 and 282 when they both elaborate on the same point that there must be wood if they choose to keep matches among their top priority items. S1 and S2 overlap immediately following S4 and S5 in lines 283 and 284, reinforcing the need to validate the assumption that there will be branches for them to use, "There's gotta be...." S4 uses an overlap in line 285 to question this assumption but not as an abrupt interruption. Rather, he productively builds on the previous speakers' contributions and introduces an element of doubt that is put out there for the group to discuss as they move forward with their decision-making, "But will there be?"

277.   S1: You need...
278.   S4:   z You need fuel. But, [what] are we gonna do? Are we gonna burn a
279.   tree =
280.   S1:   [XXX].
281.   S4: down? [Are we gonna hope that there's branches, right, right...]
282.   S5:   [There's XXX dead wood on the ground]   [XXX XXX]
283.   S1:   [We're gonna XXX but there's gotta be]
284.   S2:   [There's gotta be...]
285.   S4:   [But will there   ]
286.   be?

This discussion illustrates the way that the elements of Coates' model are used to identify the constituent parts of a collaborative style of leadership in which no one person emerges as the leader but in which leadership is shared or distributed among members of the group. To summarize, a collaborative leader uses questions to frame the interaction and to check for agreement among members, acknowledges some of the contribution of others but more commonly, builds on other statements producing smooth topic shifts, even though these contributions may overlap with those of others. Because of this fast-paced interaction aimed primarily at collaborating to produce a solution, few active listening techniques are used.

Table 3.1 provides a summary and comparison of the use of the interaction elements from Coates' model that produce each of the three distinct leadership styles discussed here.

We have analyzed five elements of discourse to provide a more detailed picture of how two key behaviors identified in traditional leadership theory emerge in actual decision-making meetings. If you recall from the discussion of traditional leadership approaches in Chapter 1, the behavioral approach proposed that leadership is composed of two general kinds of activities: task and relationship behaviors. These behaviors evolved in situational theories to stress two dimensions: directive and supportive. As can be seen in the analysis of case studies 1 and 2 as presented here, a discourse analysis approach provides a framework for identifying specific discursive elements involved in the production of both types of leaders.

Where this analysis diverges from traditional leadership theory is in the identification of the discursive elements that produce the collaborative

Table 3.1 Differences and similarities exhibited in discourse styles by leadership types

Discourse elements	Directive leader	Cooperative leader	Collaborative leader
Meaning of questions	To direct members	To solicit participation	To frame the interaction and check for agreement
Links between turns	Few	Acknowledge contribution	Some acknowledgement of contribution
Topic shifts	Abrupt	Smooth	Smooth
Listening	Minimal	Active	Minimal
Simultaneous speech	Interruptions	Few overlaps	Frequent cooperative overlaps

or what is sometimes called distributed or shared leadership approach. Shared leadership is defined as "an emergent team property that results from the distribution of leadership influence across multiple team members"[6]. The concept of shared leadership is a relatively new phenomenon in the management literature and can be contrasted with more traditional "vertical" or "hierarchical" leadership models in which the phenomenon resides predominantly within an individual rather than a group. However, the focus on teamwork in organizations has placed interest on the phenomenon of shared leadership and how it might be leveraged to increase productivity and satisfaction in these types of workplace arrangements or situations.

A fourth and somewhat related leadership style that has been identified in discourse research is the phenomenon of **co-leadership**, a construct that recognizes that leadership is rarely the preserve of one individual, but is frequently exercised by a pair of individuals, such as a top management team. Among the most well-known leadership partnerships that explicitly divide leadership roles between two or more leaders at the top of an organization are the CEO–CFO; president–vice-president; chancellor–vice-chancellor; prime minister–deputy prime minister; minister–senior civil servant; and managing director–artistic director partnerships. More recently, though, several high profile companies have chosen to divide important leadership roles between two persons. Two examples are the co-CEO-ship of John Mackey and Walter Robb, of Whole Foods Market as well as co-CEOs Yan Ness and Mike Klein at Online Tech.

At least one study has looked at the emergence of co-leadership[7]. In that study, researchers looked at how two leadership functions—task and relational maintenance activities—are actually co-performed in three different organizations. To illustrate, let's look at an extract from that study that shows how two persons in one meeting provide the same function: gathering information about the task completion. You will notice that in both instances, the speaker is using questions, an element of our previous analysis.

| Smithy: | So who's going to follow that up?...any issues that have come up since you started working on it? |
| Clara: | and IS is doing the set up for the training room, are they?...what are the issues about hitting this week's dead- um milestone?...where are the gaps likely to be? Got any other issues? |

As these examples from an actual meeting show, Smithy and Clara's questions are direct and to the point. They are the type of questions someone in authority can ask to illicit information and control the talk in the meeting by selecting both speakers and topics. In short, the use of questions in this example show a focus on task completion and how two members of a team can share a function that is typically associated with leadership.

Opportunity to Reflect

Do you think leadership communication style matters, depending on the composition of the group? If so, how? How do you think leadership communication style affects the quality of leadership in an organization? The culture of an organization? The morale and productivity of employees?

The Confounding Phenomenon of Expertise

In our research involving more than 150 participants, we observed one phenomenon that complicates a discursive approach to studies of leadership emergence: the perception of expertise. On at least two occasions, we observed that at least some of participants in the decision-making discussions had come to the process with already formed impressions regarding the expertise of their peers. Those impressions affected who was perceived to be the leader, to some extent, regardless of what was said during the meeting.

In one case, group members knew that one of them had served in the military. This service in combination with the simulation scenario—an outdoor survival situation—apparently led members to assume that this participant had the needed expertise to solve the problem presented to them and they looked to him for guidance.

In a second case, in which four of the team members were women and one was a male, one of the female participants selected the male member as the leader of the group when surveyed, presumably because it was assumed that, again, he had needed expertise to correctly solve the problem presented in the simulation. This last case is the most interesting in that videotapes of the interaction show that the male member contributed less significantly to the decision-making discussion and did not verbally produce the various elements of language that we have observed as part of leadership emergence.

These two situations illustrate what occurs when a cultural typification is evoked and its effect, or what, in this case, might be more clearly identified as a role. As was discussed in Chapter 1, the social construction of reality theory proposes that all knowledge, including the most basic, taken-for-granted commonsense knowledge of everyday reality, is derived from and maintained by social interactions. When people interact, they do so with the understanding that their respective perceptions of reality are related because they share similar experiences and values. As they act on this understanding over time, their common knowledge of reality becomes reinforced, a process which is largely invisible to the participant because he or she naturalizes the experience. Socially constructed reality is an ongoing, dynamic process; reality is reproduced by people acting on their interpretations and their knowledge of it. A **social construction** or **social construct** is any phenomenon "invented" or "constructed" by participants in a particular culture or society, existing because people agree to behave as if it exists or to follow certain conventional rules.[8] As mentioned previously, one example of a social construct is social status; that is, individuals do not naturally have greater status than others, rather it must be socially conferred.

In everyday life, we use these social constructs or what are called "typificatory schemes" to apprehend and deal with others. Thus, we comprehend another as "a father," "a mother," "a child," "an adult," "a salesperson," "a teacher," and so on. All of these typifications or roles will affect our interaction with the person to whom they are assigned. Furthermore, these roles will hold and will determine our actions in any situation, unless they are challenged in some way.

This issue is important to recognize for anyone who wants to be perceived as a leader. In other words, it is important to be aware of the social constructs that exist in a particular culture and how those social constructs might also adhere to one's person. Obviously, certain constructs can be advantageous. For example, in a particular organizational culture, holding military service may be seen as attractive in terms of leadership potential, while in others, it may be seen as a potential obstacle to be overcome.

Strategic communicators will therefore analyze their particular organizational culture and the context of communication situations to determine social constructs to attach to and whether they are advantageous or potentially a problem. Constructs that might present an obstacle will have to be challenged, likely over time, so as to change others' perceptions of the individual.

Social constructs enable us to label persons as having certain roles, such as occupational ones, but also more common designations, such as those connected to demographic characteristics such as gender, age, race, and ethnicity. The outlines of these roles also are culture specific. Chapters 5 and 6 will deal in more detail with issues related to gender and culture and the emergence of leadership.

Opportunity to Reflect

Think of a time when you or someone you know became the leader because of perceived expertise. How did that role assignment come about? Are there opportunities for you to evoke the construct of expertise to be seen as a leader in your organization or group?

Summary

This chapter illustrated how three styles of leadership emerge from the talk involved in group interactions: the directive, the cooperative, and the collaborative styles.

- A directive leader uses questions to direct agreement upon interaction participants, doesn't link his or her comments to the previous speaker's statement, makes abrupt topic shifts, uses minimal active listening techniques, tends to be verbally aggressive, and interrupts other speakers.
- A cooperative leader uses questions to solicit information or participation from others, acknowledges the position or statement of the previous speaker, avoids abrupt topic shifts, uses active listening techniques, and uses cooperative overlaps to show her support of other's ideas.

- A collaborative leader uses questions to frame the interaction and check for agreement among members, acknowledges some of the contribution of others but more commonly builds on statements to produce smooth topic shifts, even though these contributions may overlap with those of others. Because of this fast-paced interaction aimed primarily at collaborating to produce a solution, few active listening techniques are used.

One way this analysis complements traditional leadership theory is in the identification of the discursive elements that produce the collaborative or what is sometimes called distributed or shared leadership approach. Shared leadership results from the distribution of leadership influence across multiple team members. The concept of shared leadership is a relatively new phenomenon in the management literature; however, the focus on teamwork in organizations has placed interest on the phenomenon of shared leadership and how it might be leveraged to increase productivity and satisfaction. A somewhat related leadership style that has been identified in discourse research is the phenomenon of co-leadership, a construct that recognizes that leadership is rarely the preserve of one individual, but is frequently exercised by a pair of individuals, such as a top management team.

A **social construction** or **social construct** is any phenomenon "invented" or "constructed" by participants in a particular culture or society, existing because people agree to behave as if it exists or to follow certain conventional rules. In this chapter, the social construct of expertise was discussed to point out how once one is seen as a relevant expert, he or she may be attributed a leadership role, regardless of his or her communication practices.

CHAPTER 4

Leading Employees

A leader is best when people barely know he exists, when his work is done, his aim fulfilled, they will say: we did it ourselves.

—Lao Tzu

Creating Organizational Realities

Workplace settings play a critical role in the construction and enactment of members' social identities. Organizations are "mini-cultures" that provide "sources and sites of identification for individuals."[1] More specifically, organizations contribute to the construction of member identities in at least two ways: They classify members into roles that have particular meanings and they develop discursive norms from which members draw to interact with others.[2] Through these processes, organizations create leaders and subordinates.

Each organizational culture is different in the norms they provide to individuals to construct their roles. Researchers have used the concept of *communities of practice* as a means of identifying the linguistic strategies members use to negotiate organizational identity. A community of practice is an aggregate of people who come together around mutual engagement in some common endeavor. Ways of doing things, ways of talking, beliefs, values, power relations—in short, practices—emerge in the course of their joint activity around that endeavor.[3] A community of practice is different as a social construct from the traditional notion of community, primarily because it is defined simultaneously by its membership and by the practice in which that membership engages. It is the practices of the community and members' differentiated participation in them that structures the community.

Speakers develop linguistic patterns as they engage in activity in the various communities in which they participate. In actual practice, social meaning, social identity, community membership, forms of participation, the full range of community practices, and the symbolic value of linguistic form are being constantly and mutually constructed.[4] The linguistic practices of any given community of practice are continually changing as a result of the many features that come into play through the interaction of its multiple members. In particular, organizations "provide a repertoire of procedures, contracts, rules, processes, and policies" that are then incorporated by the various communities of practice "into their own practices in order to decide in specific situations what they mean in practice, when to comply with them and when to ignore them."[5] Leaders and other organizational actors draw upon this linguistic repertoire as well as the norms and values of their workplace culture to produce their discursive behaviors.

Workplace culture is a "communicative construction" that is "created and recreated as people interact over time."[6] It is a system of shared meanings and values as reflected in the discursive and behavioral norms typically displayed by members that distinguishes the group or organization from others. It should be noted that organizations may be made up of multiple subcultures that may "co-exist in harmony, conflict, or indifference to each other."[7] Workplace culture contributes significantly to the establishment of norms and expectations about leadership by defining what competent and effective leadership means.[8] The relationship between workplace culture and leadership, though, is complex in that leaders themselves also play an important role in the creation, maintenance, and change of workplace culture.[9]

Research suggests that there are seven primary characteristics that, when taken as a whole, capture the essence of an organization's culture.[10] These characteristics are summarized in Table 4.1.

Appraising the organization on each of these characteristics can provide a picture of the organization's culture and provide a framework to think about how these values are created through discourse practices.

Several studies have looked explicitly at the production of some of these characteristics in organizations. For example, Stephanie Schnurr has looked at how the use of humor can provide insights into whether an organization focuses more on rewarding and fostering teams versus individual performance (the fifth item in Table 5.1).[11] Schnurr gathered her data from three organizations involved in the information technology (IT) industry. She found that participants describing their culture as team-oriented exhibited a supportive, collaborative style of constructing

Table 4.1 Primary characteristics of organizational culture

- The degree to which employees are encouraged to be innovative and take risks.
- The degree to which employees are expected to exhibit precision, analysis, and attention to detail.
- The degree to which management focuses on results or outcomes rather than on the techniques and processes used to achieve those outcomes.
- The degree to which management decisions consider the effect of outcomes on people within the organization.
- The degree to which work activities are organized around teams or groups rather than individuals.
- The degree to which people are aggressive and competitive rather than easygoing and cooperative.
- The degree to which organizational activities emphasize maintaining the status quo compared to promoting change.

humor. In contrast, the humor used in a more individualistic culture was competitively constructed and included aggressive types of humor such as teasing.

The following excerpt from a transcript from Schnurr's study illustrates the aspects of the more individualistic interaction observed in the second organization in terms of the use of humor.[12] (The transcript has been edited for readability.)

1.	Neil:	I think there are different ways of skinning the cat, so you're not growing
2.		your own cost line and there mightbe different ways of doing that. So
3.		whatever way you decide to cut the cat, you need to know, to say, hey, how
4.		are we going to do this?
5.	Shaun:	(laughs)
6.	Victor:	You'd identify with that, Shaun?
7.	Neil:	(laughs) How we're going to do this without increasing the cost base
8.	Victor:	(laughs) Shaun's regarding the visibility.
9.	Chester:	No, Shaun can skin the cake. (laughs)
10.	Neil:	Skin the cake. Oh, yes.
11.	Victor:	There'll be no visibility to mix matters with.
12.	Neil:	Well, that wasn't a bad one, though, was it? Cut the, I said skin the cat, and
13.		cat the cake. Cut the cake and cut the cat.
14.	Victor:	(coughs)
15.	Neil:	Sorry. (laughs)
16.	Chester:	(laughs) Good attention to detail, eh?
17.	All:	(laugh)
18.	Shaun:	And that's from the guy that's had the vacation.

In this example, the humor is initiated by Victor who teasingly challenges Shaun (lines 6 and 8), thereby interrupting Neil's report and displaying his position of power in the group. Victor's humorous comment is then extended by Chester who picks up on another aspect of Neil's explanation by teasing Shaun about his love of food (line 9). He also makes fun of Neil for mixing up the idioms "skin the cat" and "cut the cake." Neil, a consultant who is new to the group, seems happy to be included in the teasing and makes a self-denigrating reply (line 10) in support of Chester's humor. As an outsider, the self-denigrating humor is a safe way of participating in the group without violating internal group rules.[13] The various topics in this sequence are then developed by individual participants until the share laughter in line 17 where the sequence might have come to an end, but Shaun, who has yet to contribute to the discussion, seems to also want to participate by adding his humorous and perhaps a little envious statement in line 18. These ending contributions also might indicate a mild form of competition between Shaun and Chester to get the last word in, which Schnurr observed in other situations in this organization.[14]

Schnurr's research is just one of a paucity of studies that look at different elements of discourse and how they construct and illuminate the culture and values of an organization. However, humor has been the focus of a good deal of research, particularly in regard to its role in leadership construction. Humor and leadership will be explored in more detail in a subsequent section of this chapter.

Opportunity to Reflect

Using the characteristics shown in Table 4.1, assess the organizational culture of your own workplace. Is it more competitive or more collaborative? What are some of the manifestations of this culture? Consider the structure of your meetings, water cooler conversations, your own interactions with colleagues, and your interactions with the boss.

"Doing" Leadership

Gail Fairhurst, a key researcher in the area of discursive leadership, has argued for an approach to leadership that views it as the management of meaning in an organizational context. Few studies, though, have attempted to show

how this actually occurs in interaction. In one such study, however, Clifton found that performing assessment during decision-making talk provides a site in which members jockey for influence in managing the meaning of organizational events.[15] This occurs through the display of *epistemic primacy.*

This study by France-based researcher Jonathan Clifton is based on the assumption that the enactment of shared meaning is visible to researchers and members alike through the notion of the next-turn proof procedure,[16] whereby the understanding of the prior turn of talk is confirmed in the next turn and so is a joint version of reality as constructed in talk. (Please see discussion in Chapter 2, "Sequential Properties of Talk and Identity Creation.")

Clifton's study is premised on the assumption that a major resource for the management of meaning is the assessment of the nature of reality as perceived by participants. This assessment of meaning is jointly arrived at by those involved. Therefore, claims regarding the nature of reality are challenged, policed, and supported by participants jockeying for influence.[17] In addition, going first also is a claim to manage meaning whereas going second can be seen as accepting another's right to manage meaning.

There are, however, different ways of going first and going second that complicate this simple equation. For example, first assessments can be "bald" or unmitigated and can be upgraded using negative interrogatives that strongly invite agreement, such as "wouldn't you agree?" They can also be downgraded through the use of modifiers, such as *looks* and *seems*, or through the use of tag questions (e.g., *right?*). Similarly, second assessments can accept the prior turn's primacy and the right of the prior speaker to claim epistemic primacy and manage meaning. Or, they can challenge the primacy of the first assessment.

The following examples are excerpted from Clifton's study and edited for readability.[18] The context of that study involved a decision-making meeting in which 18 participants were present but only 4 persons spoke. The analysis presented here will focus on a particular decision-making episode that deals with whether to screen a film called *Gas Attack* at an upcoming film festival on the opening night.[19]

1.	Chris:	One thing that I need to get everyone's opinion on for the opening gala
2.		night on the twenty first of March a great Scottish file called Gas Attack
3.		which talks about chemical weapons in Iraq and asylum seeker dispersal
4.		program in the UK.

5.	Betty:	I think we'd better check. We need to make sure we're getting strong
6.		support from headquarters.
7.	Debbie:	How did the businesses feel when you talked about Gas Attack with the
8.		sponsors?
9.	Chris:	They've yet to get back actually.
10.	Betty:	One of the things that's happened this morning is that France and Belgium
11.		blocked the NATO [resolution].
12.	Andy:	[NATO, yeah.]
13.	Betty:	It's quite monumental. I mean it is really extraordinary. We might see [not]
14.		only the
15.	Chris:	[Yeah]
16.	Betty:	beginning of the end of NATO but I think we may well be seeing another
17.		nail in Tony Blair's coffin. . . .

In this exchange, Chris introduces the topic and seeks everyone's opinion on whether to screen *Gas Attack* at the gala event. In line 5, Betty suggests getting support from headquarters before making a decision. In line 7, Debbie initiates another topic, which might move the discussion away from screening *Gas Attack*. In line 10, Betty then orients to the prior talk, skip-connecting back to her previous turn, and frames her assessment of the suggestion to screen *Gas Attack* in political terms. In doing so, she claims the first slot in an assessment sequence and so claims primacy rights to manage the meaning of the emerging decision and by doing so, "does" leadership. Andy, the legitimate power holder, does not contest this move in a second turn.

In the next example, Chris provides an alternative frame for assessing the film on the basis of artistic merit rather than in political terms.

1.	Andy:	I think that fits in the area of risk management. [yeah]
2.	Chris:	[artistically] it is a very strong
3.		film.
4.	Andy:	Yes, I can accept that [but]
5.	Betty:	[but] that's the [criteria]
6.	Chris:	[yeah]
7.	Andy:	I think we'd be sailing quite close to the breeze there so we'd have to be really
8.		really careful.
9.	Betty:	and we really can't. I mean it would be very difficult and we're going to be
10.		inviting Brian to the big opening.

In lines 4 through 10 of this example, Betty and Andy orient to Chris's challenge to their rights to manage meaning and to their leadership. In line 5, Betty completes Andy's turn—"that's the criteria"—which has the effect of claiming joint authorship of the turn, which reinforces Andy's disalignment with the artistic frame proposed by Chris. A similar pattern is followed in lines 7 through, when Andy provides an assessment and Betty adds to that assessment. In this way, she again coauthors the turn and so claims incumbency of the same identity as Andy and thus equal rights to manage meaning, assess organizational reality, and lead.[20]

Although this is a very brief exchange, it illustrates several issues related to discursive leadership. First, it shows how reality is created in an organization. In the end, through discursive means, the group effectively decided that the film *Gas Attack* should be judged politically rather than artistically. In doing so, they also talked their own organization into facticity as a primarily political rather than artistic entity. The analysis also shows how leadership involves the management of meaning through interactions with others. At the same time, it illustrates leadership that is not held by any one person but is in a constant flow and jointly held, as was discussed in Chapter 3. Finally, although, leadership is not a "property" of a person, "access to discursive resources are category-bound to more powerful roles or identities within a group or organization and this access may skew the ability to do leadership in favor" of those persons.[21] In this example, Andy, the legitimate power holder, closed the discussion of *Gas Attack* and moved to the next topic, thereby making the decision albeit implicitly.

The opening and closing of meetings as well as moving to new topics in the agenda are often the purview of the leader, typically one who has legitimate power, like Andy in the previous examples. While this is not always the case, it tends to be so because a meeting is a type of genre and thus has certain rules that are expected to be followed by participants. (Genre is the term for any category of text, whether written or spoken, audial or visual, that is based on some set of stylistic criteria.)

Opportunity to Reflect

Can you think of a situation in your workplace when you or someone else attempted to define a particular reality? If the attempt was successful, why? If not, how might the interaction have been changed, if at all, to impact the outcome?

Facework and Performance Appraisals

Erving Goffman is an important contributor to current thinking on certain approaches to discourse studies and is widely considered the most influential sociologist in the 20th century. In Goffman's major work, *The Presentation of the Self in Everyday Life*, he describes the theatrical performances that occur in face-to-face interactions. He holds that when an individual comes in contact with another person, he attempts to control or guide the impression that the other person will form of him, by altering his own setting, appearance, and manner.[22] At the same time, the person that the individual is interacting with attempts to form an impression of and obtain information about the individual. Goffman also believed that participants in social interactions engage in certain practices to avoid embarrassing themselves or others. This is called *facework*.

Goffman's concept of face has been further established by a number of researchers in the area of discourse as an emergent property of talk-in-interaction and a relational phenomenon rather than a psychological one. The issue of face has further developed into a theory of politeness that has been used extensively by researchers of humor in interaction. It is also a concern for those who work in the area of multi- and cross-cultural interactions, since cultures are believed to value face differently from one another. (This latter issue will be discussed in more detail in Chapter 5.)

The concept of face is addressed here because an important part of most managers' jobs is to assess the performance of subordinates. In the growing number of organizations that use teams, assessment of peers and superiors is often accomplished using what is commonly referred to as the 360-degree method. Performance appraisals are generally considered delicate situations in which the face of the participants is at stake, and thus, skillful facework is required to retain social cohesion and ensure the maintenance of a good working relationship.

Clifton's study illustrates how this facework occurs through a variety of discourse strategies.[23] Excerpts from that study are used here to identify and illustrate those strategies. (Excerpts have been edited for readability.) The following is an example of a *presequence* (shown in underline), which is used to introduce the topic, the first question on the appraisal form.

Andy:	<u>What I have to actually try and complete on</u> the final document is where we think you can go this year.

Presequences prior to questions can display orientation to the forth-coming action as delicate.[24] In addition to the use of a presequence in this example, Andy starts on a personal footing through the use of "I" and then later calls on his institutional identity through the use of "we." This move presents the task as a reticent action that he must perform as part of an institutional task. He is thus able to present a possible face threat as if it were committed by an anonymous organization rather than by himself.[25]

In the response, Bob doesn't immediately address the known but unspoken question—"what are your career ambitions? Specify action which would provide for your longer term development"—but builds up to it as underlined in the following example:

> Bob: I feel I can do the job I'm in now. When I came in, I needed a bit of learning, and obviously, I can improve. You can carry on improving and improving, but I find very much that the job is in my scope and as I say, I feel that now is the time that I ought to be preparing for the next step. That's personally how I see this coming year. I feel certain specific areas of weakness. I know to move up to the next step, I must fill in those. <u>I'm hoping the company can provide that sort of training and experience.</u>

By displacing his answer to the question to the end of the turn and prefacing it with an account, Bob is attempting to resolve a possible threat to face by focusing on "no fault considerations."[26] The consideration of no fault applies to both himself and the appraiser. First, Bob must display an identity that has "weaknesses" that justify the consideration of training, but at the same time, protect his face by showing that he is also competent. He does this by being vague, "I feel certain specific areas of weakness."

In Andy's response to the request, rather than stating a direct disagreement and a possible threat to face, he suggests an alternative:

> Andy: Rather than actually working in that department, you could spend a bit of time in industrial engineering, for instance.
> Bob: Yes, I mean, it's a [possibility]
> Andy: [another] area we could perhaps develop is a job rotation or just exposure to during the year.
> Bob: yeah. [I mean]
> Andy: [BUT] I agree. I think you are tending to take the job rather in your stride. . .

Bob replies with a weak agreement and Andy orients to this statement as projecting disagreement, so he makes a further suggestion so as to avoid disagreement. Bob's response, "yeah, I mean," is again interpreted by Andy as a preface to disagreement, so he heads it off by speaking more loudly and validating Bob's self-assessment. This is an example of how participants work together to allow Andy to reformulate statements so as to avoid disagreement and maintain face for both interactants.

In the development of the discussion, Bob returns to a discussion of his weaknesses:

Bob:	Other things that I feel weak on as regards the next step, I've had no real experience in marketing and sales. Whether there's any chance of getting that sort of experience
Andy:	You mean not as a possible career move but as
Bob:	No, as a broadening of my experience.
Andy:	Exposure to that
Bob:	Some exposure to it. I know I think I have a rather traditional view of what marketing do. It's a rather rosy life and occasionally they make some decisions that affect us and make life difficult
Andy:	Well, I'm guessing they may like to entertain you for a couple of weeks and show you what hard work really is
	(both laugh)

This example sets up an "us versus them" dichotomy, which, by allowing Andy and Bob to be co-incumbents of the same identity (production men), builds solidarity and so minimizes face threats. The laughter shows recognition of Andy's final utterance as "improper talk, which marks a move toward intimate interaction and so seeks to build positive social solidarity and so does positive facework."[27]

These examples show some of the discursive strategies that institutional actors can use to work together to preserve each other's positive face, and more specifically, how this is done in a performance appraisal context. This work is achieved implicitly rather than directly through the moves each actor makes in the discussion.

Opportunity to Reflect

Identify some talk you have used to avoid threatening the face of others. What other strategies might you incorporate into your repertoire? Would they be judged as appropriate in your organization or group? Why or why not?

Humor, Leadership, and Facework

Humor serves a wide range of functions at work. One of the most important functions of humor is to construct and maintain good relations with fellow workers. In other words, humor is a very effective means of "doing collegiality" at work. Humor is advocated as a means of improving productivity, for instance, and an essential tool for managers, especially in meetings. It can be used to strengthen collegiality or bonds of friendship or to soften an instruction or a criticism. It can be used to release tension or defuse anger. In some cases, the instigator of the humor may sometimes be more amused than the target or the audience. Humor can provide a camouflage for an astringent, disparaging comment or even take the form of a direct face attack and insult; barbed humor and jocular abuse are frequent in some contexts.[28]

While humor is generally intended to amuse, it may also serve to hedge face-threatening acts, such as directives, criticisms, and insults.[29] In interactions where relative power is particularly salient, however, humor may be used repressively by the powerful to maintain authority and control, while continuing to appear collegial. Alternatively, it may be used by subordinates to challenge control, encoding a criticism in a socially acceptable form and making the negative communicative intent less obvious.[30]

More recently, researchers have begun to treat humor as a one source of insight into the complexity of the workings of business organizations as was illustrated in an earlier section of this chapter, "Creating Organizational Realities." In a related vein, Holmes and Marra identified elements of humor used in two differing styles of leadership as identified by psychological leadership theory and the transactional and transformative leadership theory (See Chapter 1).[31] Table 4.2 lists the characteristics of each of these leadership types.

Table 4.2 Transactional versus transformational leadership

Transactional	Transformational
Focus on goals and related rewards	Charismatic, inspirational, visionary
Focus on contractual obligations	Intellectually stimulating
Monitors mistakes and deviations from norms	Encourages creativity and questioning
Corrective response to errors and problems	Reliable, trustworthy, ethical model

As Table 4.2 indicates, a transactional approach tends to focus on maintaining the status quo, emphasizing norms, roles, and responsibilities. Humor oriented to sustaining and maintaining power and status relationships is clearly a useful resource when this style of leadership is adopted.[32] Humor serves to make more palatable both directive utterances that emphasize organizational responsibilities and critical comments that address deviations from norms.

However, humor that reinforces group boundaries and strengthens team solidarity could be seen as sustaining the status quo, emphasizing the in-group and maintaining conservative boundaries at the expense of innovation. Humor oriented to solidarity and to power can thus be perceived as resources for instantiating a transactional leadership style, reinforcing the status quo, emphasizing institutional roles and responsibilities, and affirming institutional values.[33]

Conversely, a transformational style of leadership encourages creativity and innovation, the contesting of old assumptions, and questioning of established ways of doing things. Humor used to "create team" illustrates how it is part of the construction of a transformational leadership style. Leaders who encourage a high-energy, brainstorming approach to an issue or a problem also tend to encourage and contribute to the sparky, humorous sequences that often lead to bursts of creative mental and intellectual activity.[34]

Humor Oriented to Solidarity

We will examine two types of humor that can be used to promote solidarity: One that is more spontaneous and jointly created and a second that is more competitive in nature.

"Creating Team"

In the following example, the transformational team leader supports and extends humor and actively contributes to the interactive, high energy style that characterizes the sequence.[35] The context of the discussion is a planning meeting of a group of regional managers in New Zealand, and the humor revolves around the advantages and disadvantages of living in a small town. (The excerpt is taken from the Holmes and Marra study and has been edited for readability.)

1. Tina:	the fact that we don't go to Malt [doesn't mean that people from Malt can't go	
2.	somewhere to get help 'cuz they were interested enough t-	
3. Ray:	if you live in Malt you need to go somewhere to get help	
4.	[General laughter]	
5. Scott:	there is actually quite a big consultancy in Malt	
6. Tom:	is there?	
7. Scott:	yeah	
8. Hal:	I was told many years ago that Malt was the	
9. Kay:	heart of the wife-swapping area for [name of province]	
10. Scott:	isn't it Malt that had the highest rate of um oh no that's Stout	
11. Tina:	ex nuptial births	
12. Scott:	the highest rate per capita	
13. Scott:	Malt or Stout [laughs]	
14. Kay:	did they?	
15. Tina:	rates of ex nuptial births at one point . . .	
16. Mel:	it's the alcohol that does it	
17.	[General laughter and overlapping talk throughout next section]	
18. Tina:	poor old Malt	
19. Kay:	we should be there	
20. Tina:	we should be there	
21. Scott:	what do you want more children?	
22	[General laughter] . . .	
23. Scott:	an outpost.	
24. Tina:	an outpost we want an outpost in Malt	
25. Scott:	right okay	
26. Tina:	open an outpost in Malt. How far is Malt from Halty?	
27. Scott:	I don't know 'cuz I always bypass it and do the back road. It's such an awful	
28.	place.	
29.	[General laughter]\	

In this example, participants work together to supportively develop the topic at length, making more and more outrageous claims about the challenges of life in a small town. Each contribution supports and further develops the proposition of the previous contributor. The style is energetic: there is a great deal of fast and frequently overlapping speech, as well as laughter throughout.[36] The contributions are closely integrated discursively, with requests for confirmation and a repetition of single words and phrases to whole clauses ("we should be there"). This episode of collaborative humor serves the useful purpose of actively constructing group cohesion and strengthening the sense of rapport between the group of regional managers who meet only irregularly.

Competitive Humor

In some communities of practice, constructing a sense of team and emphasizing group cohesion is achieved by a more competitive style of humor.[37] Becoming a member of such a group involves learning to fit in and participate in the exchange of humorous insults and barbed witty comments.[38] In the following example, Bob, the team leader, has let one of his team members take the blame for not picking up on a particular point near the end of a long report.

1. Eric:	[smiling voice]: Bob sees those sorts of things too, by the way, notice that
3. All:	[laugh]
4. Bob:	I don't read them through [laughs] I rely on you guys to read them.

In the example, Eric points out in a humorous tone that Bob, the team leader, has also missed the error they have criticized another team member for. Rather than accepting the critical comment, Bob responds with a humorous retort, claiming he doesn't read the reports. As this exchange illustrates, this particular contestive style serves to create and establish good rapport between the team members. What should be noted is that this style works for this team; it may not work for others, which underscores the importance of situating talk within a particular community of practice.

Humor Oriented to Power

A second broad category of workplace humor orients to the power dimension by addressing participants' need to maintain "face" or self-esteem.[39] Humor used this way functions to protect the addressees' as well as the speaker's dignity. In this capacity, humor may be used to mitigate "unwelcome news" in a variety of forms. According to Holmes and Marra, there are three sub-categories of this function of humor:

- Humor as a mitigator of instructions from a superior to a subordinate
- Humor that softens a critical comment

- Humor that mitigates an admission of error or undignified behavior[40]

In the context of an interaction between a leader and a subordinate, the first two focus on the addressee's or subordinate's face needs, while the third is oriented to the leader's need to maintain a dignified profile. Illustrative dialogs for each category are taken from the work of Homes and Marra.

Humor As a Mitigator of Instructions From a Superior to a Subordinate

Humor is an effective discourse strategy for reducing the face threat of a directive or instruction to a workplace colleague.[41] While this is especially true if the addressee is an equal or superior in status, it is equally useful to leaders in giving directives to subordinates and followers. In the following example, members of a project team are discussing how they will respond when the call center they are establishing is up and running.[42]

1. Troy:	Yeah , well, we've got the four temps	
2. Kay:	There'll be so many people grabbing the phone	
3. Troy:	Plenty of people	
4. Ann:	Do you want us to be in there as well?	
5. Kay:	Well, I think you'll be sitting at your desks, won't you, doing your jobs?	
7.	(lots of laughter and people talking at the same time) . . .	
8.	I think it's important for you guys to do your jobs rather than be supporting the	
9.	people and stepping back and observing what's going on	

Kay's response to Ann's question in line 4 is to indicate clearly that she does not expect the team members to stand around watching the center operators answering the phones. Her light and slightly arch tone conveys the message with humor, but, as illustrated by the fact that she proceeds to repeat it in a more serious tone (lines 8–9), there is no doubt that this is an instance where the team leader is conveying instructions to her team.

Humor That Softens a Critical Comment

Similarly, humor is useful in reducing the sting of a required criticism or negative evaluative comment. Humor provides socially acceptable packaging for the necessary but, from the addressee's perspective, unpalatable message.[43] In these situations, tone of voice is often helpful in "cuing" the humorous intention.[44]

In the example that follows, two advisors are comparing written evaluations; Andy, a more senior and experienced person, implies that Vince has been too wordy in a written report.[45]

1. Andy:	And apart from that, I've just got what you've got, but in a lot less words.
2.	[both laugh]

Andy conveys the fundamentally negative message that Vince's report is too wordy and verbose, but by using humor, Andy softens the negative impact, paying attention to the need to maintain Vince's dignity.

Humor That Mitigates an Admission of Error or Undignified Behavior

A third type of power-oriented humor is that that mitigates an admission of error or undignified behavior, helping the leader to maintain face and a dignified profile. When a person in a position of power and authority makes an error, humor can provide a way of reducing the embarrassment of the gaffe, attenuating its negative impact on the leader's persona.[46]

In the following example Clara misinterprets a humorous comment as referring to her own mother, rather than the British Queen Mother, but recovers quickly and exploits her mistake to generate more humor. Clara is often jokingly referred to by her team as Queen Clara.[47]

1. Sam:	How's your mum?
2. Clara:	Sorry?
3. Sam:	She broke her hip, didn't she?
4. Clara:	my mother?
5. All:	(laugh) (laughter continues)
6. Clara:	What are you talking about?
7. Sid:	(laughs) The queen mother:
8. Clara:	Oh
9. All:	(laugh)
10. Clara:	My husband and I (in a parody of a British Royal accent) are confident that she
12. All:	(laugh)
13.	will pull through.
14. All:	(laugh)

Clara successfully survives her misunderstanding without embarrassing herself. In fact, she turns the situation to her advantage and manages to reinforce and emphasize her authoritative position as "Queen" with her quick-witted response to the humorous scenario that her team has constructed.

These examples taken together illustrate ways in which leaders use the diverse functions of humor. It is clearly a useful discursive resource, available to effective leaders in managing the potential problems around power and authority differentials in the workplace. In order to achieve workplace goals, those in positions of power need to issue directives, make critical comments, and maintain a dignified demeanor that will earn respect. Humor can assist in "doing power" in an acceptable way in a society or workplace culture that values collegiality and resents heavy-handed authoritarianism.

Opportunity to Reflect

Think of your interactions with your boss or your subordinates. How is humor used? Are these instances of humor oriented toward solidarity or power? Think of your own or your subordinates' reaction to humor. Was the humor successful in accomplishing its task?

Leadership and Managing Conflict in Meetings

Thus far, this chapter has explored the importance of understanding the community of practice in helping leaders to determine the communication behaviors that are likely to be more successful in any particular context, how leadership emerges in talk, the importance of face in discussions of workplace dynamics, and how humor can be used as a face-saving strategy. This section deals with another common challenge of effective leaders: Managing conflict.

A good deal of research has been done on conflict, both in communication and in traditional management and leadership studies. One of the more well known of these is the work of Rahim and Bonama that identified five conflict management styles: Collaborating, accommodating, compromising, avoiding, and competing.[48] From a discourse perspective,

many studies have emphasized the importance of context when consider-
ing conflict, an assumption in line with the opening discussion found
in this chapter of the value of understanding a particular community of
practice and its impact on what should and should not be said. It has been
argued that differences in setting[49] as well as culture[50] have an impact on
the enactment of disagreement.

Again, we turn to Holmes and Marra, whose research in the Wellington Workplace Project in New Zealand is recognized arguably as the most
productive endeavor undertaken in discourse research to examine workplace practices. In their study of conflict, they found that effective managers clearly adopt a range of different strategies in different contexts.[51] In
this study, they identified four strategies along a continuum from least to
most confrontational:

- Conflict avoidance—asserting the "agenda"
- Conflict diversion—moving conflict out
- Conflict resolution using negotiation—working through
  conflict
- Conflict resolution using authority—imposing a decision

These strategies as defined by Holmes and Marra will be explained in the
sections that follow.

Conflict Avoidance: Asserting the "Agenda"

Conflict can arise in meetings when there are differences in participants'
understandings of what they are supposed to be discussing or decid-
ing, or when participants have different views of what has been agreed.
Constructive steps, such as setting a clear agenda, summarizing progress,
keeping the discussion on track, and explicitly verbalizing and ratifying
implicit decisions, are therefore important strategic moves that contribute
to maintaining order and avoiding conflict.

One of the most common strategies for meeting management is simply to stick to the agenda. When a digression promises to introduce contentious but irrelevant material, this can be a useful conflict-avoidance
tactic. Phrases such as *to get back to the agenda* and *just moving on* regularly
occur in meetings as explicit discourse markers of this tactic. Holmes and
Marra found that in situations where the meeting Chair was someone

other than the team manager, he or she would on occasion "move the meeting along" by overtly indicating that it was time to move to the next agenda item. These short intrusions by the meeting chair were always strategic moves to get the meeting back on track, but on occasion they also served to divert discussion from contentious areas that the leader judged irrelevant to the primary objectives of the meeting.

In the following example from that study, a very effective leader, Clara, manages the opening of a meeting, which includes a covert challenge to her authority.

1. Clara:	Okay, well, we might just start without Seth. He can come in and can review	
2.	the minutes from last week	
3. Renee:	Are you taking the minutes this week?	
4. Clara:	No, I'm just trying to chair the meeting. Who would like to take minutes this	
5.	week?	
6. Renee:	Who hasn't taken the minutes yet?	
7. Ben:	I haven't yet. I will.	
8. Clara:	Thank you, Benny.	
9. Renee:	Oh, Benny takes beautiful minutes, too.	
10. Ben:	Don't tell them. They'll want me doing it every week.	
11.	[general laughter]	
12. Clara:	It's a bit of a secret. Okay, shall we kick off and just go round the room doing an	
13.	update? And then when Seth comes in with minutes, we need to check on any	
14.	action items from our planning. Over to you, Marlene.	

Clara declares the meeting open, *we might just start* (line 1), even though one of the members is not present. She then ducks Renee's attempt to get her to take minutes by asserting her role as Chair (line 4), and then asks for a volunteer for this task (lines 4–5). She approves Benny as minute taker, and sets the agenda for the meeting (lines 12–14). Finally, she allocates the first turn, *over to you Marlene* (line 15).

This excerpt illustrates Clara's skill in managing potential conflict. Renee challenges Clara's role as leader by attempting to take on that role herself by asking whether she will take the minutes. This challenge further evidenced when she takes over from Clara the responsibility for allocating the role of minute-taker by asking for someone who has not already undertaken this duty (line 6) and approving Benny as a suitable volunteer (line 9). Clara, however, manages Renee's contesting behavior good-humoredly but firmly. She re-asserts her role at line 8 by ratifying Benny as minute-taker, and then after a brief acknowledgment of the humorous exchange between Renee and Benny, she very firmly announces the agenda with *okay shall we kick off and just go round the room doing an update?* (line 13).

This is a brief example of one of the more subtle ways in which effective leaders manage potential conflict by using their meeting management skills to defuse and divert it.

Conflict Diversion: Moving Conflict Out

A second effective strategy for managing conflict or potential conflict is to simply divert it to a different context. In the Holmes and Marra study, this tactic was found to be used predominantly in two related kinds of situations:

- When it became clear that a particular issue needed further exploration or preparatory work before it was reasonable for meeting participants to discuss it.
- When a disagreement arose between two experts or perhaps a sub-group about an (often technical) issue that was not strictly part of the business of the meeting as a whole.

In such cases, effective leaders typically identified the issue and then diverted it to another venue for discussion as is shown in the following example:

1. Barb:	Mobile's different, though, isn't it?	
2. Eric:	I don't know. We're still working on that.	
3. Barb:	Are we still doing history?	
4. Eric:	The original said no, there wasn't any history, which I said didn't make sense	
5.	'cause it was all available, so I should check [coughs]	
7. Barb:	mm	
8. Mark:	But it seems like the questions and answers from the [name] feed when there	
9.	wasn't any data there either.	
10. Cal:	That one certainly was a known, Mark.	
11. Mark:	Yeah [laughs] so yeah	
12. Eric:	yeah	
13. Mark:	That was known	
14. Cal:	Yes	
15. Mark:	Okay, well	
16. Cal:	Yep	
17. Barb:	Okay, well you guys need to talk about it tomorrow not now.	
18. Mark:	We'll talk. Yep.	

In this typical example of a problem gradually emerging from a discussion, it becomes apparent that the area of contention is something that needs to be resolved by the experts, and that there is no point in pursuing the discussion further until it is resolved.

Conflict Resolution Using Negotiation: Working Through Conflict

A third strategy for dealing with areas of disagreement in meetings is to acknowledge them and then "manage" them rather than avoid or divert them. This approach generally involves negotiating consensus among participants. Good chairs and effective leaders tended to adopt this strategy in the Holmes and Marra study, particularly when the decision was a serious or important one, that is, one that set a precedent for subsequent decisions.

In the following situation taken from that study, a team is involved in a discussion of the allocation of responsibilities that relate to a range of tasks that intersected with complicated staffing problems. The need to catch up with the filing had become a particular problem and a number of possible solutions were discussed, some involving complicated re-assignment of duties.[52] One possible solution, first proposed at a relatively early point in the meeting, was to bring in external people to do the filing. A relatively senior team member was not happy with this suggestion, and throughout the discussion she raised a variety of objections to it whenever it reemerged, as it regularly did. The manager, Leila, handled the contentious issue by encouraging extensive and explicit discussion. Finally, she checked that all were happy with the proposed solution.

The following excerpts from that discussion show some of the ways that Leila sought consensus:

Leila:	I mean, we may not be able to find a solution but, I mean, you're the people who are in the best situation for knowing that. What's your feeling?
Leila:	I want people to be honest about whether they, if they don't, you know, even if things come up again. Now if you don't feel comfortable say so..
Leila	You need to work that through
Leila:	Does this feel okay? I mean I don't want anyone to feel that

Leila's strategies of requesting people to make explicit their reservations and overtly seeking agreement before proceeding finally resulted in a satisfactory conclusion.

Conflict Resolution Using Authority: Imposing a Decision

Finally, leaders have available the tactic of direct confrontation with the overt assertion and imposition of what they want. Because of their positions of power, they can ignore, discount and over-ride the views of others, and insist that what they want goes. However, Holmes and Marra found the use of this tactic rare. Leaders who ignore the views of their team members take a risk by doing so.

In the following example, a team is discussing the form the initial greeting on the organization's answering phone should take. The leader Clara's response on this issue is uncompromising.

1. Sam:	We were going to have a vote on "welcome" or "kia ora"
2. Clara:	Oh, it's "welcome."
3. Sam:	You sure?
4. Clara:	Yes.
5. Peg:	You phone up and say whatever you want to outside business hours
7. Vita:	(laugh)
8. Peg:	But in business hours it's "welcome."

Clara firmly assert her decision, "*welcome*" (line 3), and the team clearly accepts her decision, although with a wry humorous comment from Peg to soften the impact of the direct and explicit challenge to Sam's proposal that the issue be decided democratically by a vote (line 1).

In summary, Holmes and Marra's study found that the extent to which the participants worked together on a regular basis and formed a tight-knit versus a loosely-knit community of practice seemed to be a potentially relevant factor in the choice of strategy for managing conflict. Leaders of closely-knit teams seemed more likely to adopt a strategy of negotiation and to avoid direct confrontation. People who did not work regularly together were more willing to engage in directly confrontational discourse.

In addition, the importance or seriousness of the issue had an effect on the tactics used. Some contentious issues can be avoided, ignored, or diverted to another context for resolution elsewhere. Holmes and Marra found that experienced leaders provided explicit guidance on which issues were to be discussed at the meeting and which were not; they typically kept people on track with discussion, and they clearly selected the areas of conflict that they were prepared to discuss at length and those they were not. In general, issues that merited fuller discussion were ones with serious consequences for the organization.

Finally, another factor that may affect the way that conflict is handled is the leadership style adopted by the leader in each meeting. Holmes and Marra found that some leaders tended to construct themselves as "team players," while others tended to be more individualistic, performing as "hero leaders." This leadership construction was apparent in such areas as the extent to which a leader drew attention to his or her leadership role, the insistence on steady progress through the agenda, and the importance of clear decisions as a primary responsibility associated with the leader's role.

Good leadership requires skills in relational practices, such as taking account of the relationships between people at work and the face needs of others in the interaction. Because of this, disagreement and conflict is typically "negotiated" and worked through dynamically, often over several speaker turns, but sometimes throughout a long meeting, and in some cases even over several meetings.

Opportunity to Reflect

What is your own strategy of managing conflict? Can you reflect on it and assess its efficiency? Has it been successful in moving your team forward? Do you find yourself switching between different strategies? What factors influence your choices of conflict management strategy?

Summary

Workplace settings pay a critical role in the construction and enactment of members' social identities. Organizations contribute to the construction of member identities in at least two ways: They classify members into roles that have particular meanings and they develop discursive norms from which members draw to interact with others. Through these processes, organizations create leaders and subordinates.

Each organizational culture is different in the norms that they provide to individuals to construct their roles. Researchers have used the concept of communities of practice as a means of identifying the linguistic strategies members employ to negotiate organizational identity.

A community of practice is an aggregate of people who come together around mutual engagement in some common endeavor. Ways of doing things, ways of talking, beliefs, values, power relations—in short, practices—emerge in the course of their joint activity around that endeavor.

The linguistic strategies of any given community of practice will be continually changing as a result of the many features that come into play through the interaction of its multiple members.

In particular, organizations provide a repertoire of procedures, contracts, rules, processes, and policies that are then incorporated by the various communities of practice into their own practices in order to decide in specific situations what they mean, when to comply with them, and when to ignore them. Leaders and other organizational actors draw upon this linguistic repertoire as well as the norms and values of their workplace culture to produce their discursive behaviors.

Through discursive means, groups talk their own organizations into facticity. Leadership involves the management of meaning through interactions with others; it is not necessarily held by any one person, is in a constant flow, and can be jointly held. Finally, although, leadership is not a "property" of a person, access to discursive resources are category-bound to more powerful roles or identities within a group or organization, and this access may skew the ability to "do leadership" in favor of those persons.

Humor serves multiple functions in the workplace. This chapter illustrated five ways that humor might be used, with two types oriented to solidarity and three types of humor oriented to power. Humor can be oriented to solidarity by "creating team." Humor can also be used to build power, serving as a mitigator of instructions from a superior to a subordinate, softening a critical comment, or mitigating an admission of error or undignified behavior.

Finally, four strategies used by managers to manage conflict were discussed. Ranging along a continuum from least to most confrontational, these were conflict avoidance or asserting the "agenda," conflict diversion or moving conflict out, conflict resolution using negotiation or working through conflict, and conflict resolution using authority or imposing a decision.

CHAPTER 5

Cross-Cultural Leadership

Effective leadership is not about making speeches or being liked; leadership is defined by results not attributes.

—Peter Drucker

As previously suggested, culture has an important effect on communication practices. **Culture** is defined as the learned set of beliefs, values, rules, norms, symbols, and traditions that are common to a group of people. It is a way of life, customs, and script for a group of people.[1] As we explored in Chapter 1, culture is a social construction. That is, it is produced by the communication practices (thought broadly as the use of symbols to make meaning) that become routinized by groups or communities of people.

In the United States, the study of culture began in earnest in the 1960s with research on ethnic and racial identities; it has since expanded to look at differences among people of different countries, societies, and regional groups. In the past few decades, many studies have focused on identifying and classifying the basic values of different cultures. Each produced greater understanding of cultural differences, but each also had its limitations and critics. However, understanding these concepts can provide us some insight into cultural differences and how they may affect our communication effectiveness. As an opening then to this chapter, key studies of culture will be reviewed to provide a foundation for understanding cultural differences. Following that review, findings of studies will be summarized that consider the interaction of culture with leadership. The chapter will conclude with a discussion of the use of discourse methods to look at leadership and culture.

Hofstede's Cultural Dimensions

Perhaps the most referenced study of culture is the research of Geert Hofstede. Hofstede analyzed questionnaires obtained from more than

100,000 respondents in more than 50 countries and identified five major dimensions on which cultures differ: power distance, uncertainty avoidance, individualism–collectivism, masculinity–femininity, and long-term versus short-term orientation:[2]

- **Power distance** is based on different values that society places on equality and hierarchy. Low power distance means that society is more egalitarian; people tend to be self-directed, roles are flexible, and power and authority can be challenged. Austria, Israel, Denmark, New Zealand, and Ireland are considered low power distance countries. High power distance means more hierarchical structures exist with strong limitations for behaviors appropriate for certain roles. Power and status are not to be questioned and directions are taken from above. Malaysia, Panama, Guatemala, the Philippines, and Mexico are examples of high power distance countries. The United States falls somewhere in-between the two groups and has greater equality among different societal levels.

- **Uncertainty avoidance** refers to a cultural group's tolerance for uncertainty and ambiguity. Low uncertainly avoidance means that people are more comfortable changing plans, there are few rules and regulations, and decisions are made quickly with little information. The United States, Australia, Hong Kong are examples of low **uncertainty** avoidance countries. Countries such as Japan, France, Spain are high on the uncertainty avoidance scale and generally are more cautious, change slowly, and avoid risks.

- **Individualism versus collectivism: In individualistic cultures,** the autonomy of the individual is of paramount importance, whereas commitment to the group is most important in **collectivist cultures**. The individualism–collectivism continuum is thought by some scholars to be the most important dimension that distinguishes one culture from another.[3] The United States ranks number one in individualism. Venezuela is the most collectivist of countries, with Mexico, Thailand, Singapore, and Japan also ranking on the collectivist side of

Table 5.1 Characteristics of individualist versus collectivist cultures

Individualistic cultures	Collectivist cultures
Value individual freedom; place "I" before "we."	Value the group over the individual; Place "we" before "I."
Value independence.	Value commitment to family, tribe, and clan.
Value competition over cooperation.	Value cooperation over competition.
Value telling the truth over sparing feelings.	Value "saving face" by not causing embarrassment.
Examples: United States, Australia, Great Britain, Canada, Netherlands	*Examples*: Venezuela, Pakistan, Peru, Taiwan, Thailand

the continuum.[4] Approximately 70% of the world's population lives in collectivist cultures.[5] Table 5.1 summarizes the characteristics of individualistic and collectivist cultures.

- **Masculinity versus femininity.** In this dimension, masculine cultures emphasize achievement and economic growth and have distinct gender roles, whereas a feminine culture has more flexible gender roles and emphasizes nurturance and quality of work life. Middle Eastern cultures tend to be more masculine while Scandinavian countries tend to be feminine. The United States also ranks fairly high in masculinity.

- **Long-term versus short-term orientation.** Values associated with long-term orientation are thrift and perseverance; values associated with short-term orientation include short- to medium-term planning, focus on spending, and personal survival. The United States, the United Kingdom, and Germany fall within the short-term orientation. China, Brazil, Japan are long-term orientation cultures.

It should be noted that Hofstede's work has been criticized for, among other things, presenting an overly static model that doesn't recognize individual differences in cultural performance. However, it is useful in providing a conceptual framework for thinking about cultural differences.

Because of the saliency of the individualist–collectivist distinction, two additional concepts related to this distinction have been developed. These are low-context versus high-context cultures and face negotiation theory. (The issue of facework was introduced in Chapter 4 but is developed here in a bit more detail to highlight its importance regarding cultural differences.)

Low- Versus High-Context Cultures

Anthropologist Edward T. Hall gave us another way to look at cultural difference in terms of high and low context. Individualist and collectivist cultures emphasize different kinds of communication. People in collectivist cultures pay a great deal of attention to the context of the communication rather than the explicit, transmitted code or words. For example, in Japan, Korea, China, and Arab and Latin American countries, a good deal of time is spent in relationship building—formal communication and getting acquainted—before business takes place and intentions are stated. In contrast, low-context cultures pay more attention to the explicit code or words than to the context. In the United States, Switzerland, Germany, and Scandinavian countries, people get to the point and clearly state what they want.

Table 5.2 shows examples of low-context versus high-context cultural characteristics.

These cultural differences also can affect how people perceive verbal and nonverbal cues. Those from low-context, individualistic cultures tend to pay more attention to verbal messages, whereas those from high-context, collectivist cultures tend to pay more attention to nonverbal messages.

Table 5.2 *Characteristics of low- and high-context cultures*

Low-context Northern Europe, North America	High-context *Japan, Saudi Arabia, Mediterranean Europe, Latin America*
• Less formality • Direct, explicit communication • Get right to business • Need larger personal space	• Very formal • Indirect, implicit communication • Build a relationship and trust before conducting business • Comfortable with little personal space (Latin America, Saudi Arabia)

The context orientation of various subcultures and social groups within the United States varies. For example, those of the African American culture tend to be more collectivist and high-context than do Caucasians from European descent; and working-class people tend to be more collectivist and high context than do white-collar professionals.

Face Negotiation Theory

Face negotiation theory was first postulated by Stella Ting-Toomey in 1985 to explain how different cultures manage conflict and communicate. The theory has gone through multiple iterations since that time. In essence, the theory explains that the root of conflict is based on identity management at the individual and cultural levels. The various facets of individual and cultural identities are described as *faces*, the public images of an individual or group that the society sees and evaluates based on cultural norms and values. Conflict occurs when a group or individual's face is threatened. This can occur in two directions: embarrassing another can make individuals of certain cultures uncomfortable since this entails a potential act of impoliteness. Conversely, saving one's own face, or avoiding embarrassing one's self, can also be a concern.

Many different strategies and factors affect how cultures manage identity. Ting-Toomey argues that the face of the group in collectivist cultures is more important than the face of any individual in that group. In individualist cultures, the face of the individual is more important than the face of the group. Furthermore, there are small- and large-power distances associated with each culture. A small-power-distance culture believes that authority is earned, power is distributed equally, and everyone's opinion matters. The individual is highly valued, as in the United States, for example. In large-power-distance cultures, authority is inherited, power is from top to bottom, and the boss is infallible. The good of the group is valued.

The GLOBE Studies

The Global Leadership and Organizational Behavior Effectiveness (GLOBE) research program incorporated Hofstede's cultural dimensions and Implicit Leadership Theory (ITL) into one study designed to measure whether certain leadership styles translate across cultures. The ILT asserts that people's underlying assumptions, stereotypes, beliefs, and schemas influence the extent to which they view someone as a good leader. Since people across cultures tend to hold different implicit beliefs, schemas, and stereotypes, it would seem only natural that their underlying beliefs in what makes a good leader differ across cultures.[6]

The GLOBE study involved more than 160 investigators who used quantitative methods to study the responses of 17,000 managers in more than 950 organizations representing 62 cultures. The researchers divided the data from the 62 countries into 10 regional clusters and identified nine cultural dimensions: uncertainty avoidance, power distance, institutional collectivism, in-group collectivism, gender egalitarianism, assertiveness, future orientation, performance orientation, and humane orientation.[7] Some of those dimensions correlate with the respective dimension from Hofstede, but they differ in that the GLOBE dimensions distinguish between cultural values and cultural practices:

- **Uncertainty avoidance** refers to the extent to which a cultural group relies on established social norms, rituals, and procedures to avoid uncertainty.
- **Power distance** refers to the degree to which members of a cultural group expect and agree that power should be shared unequally.
- **Institutional collectivism** describes the degree to which a cultural group encourages institutional or societal collective action. It is concerned with whether cultures identify with broader societal interests rather than with individual goals.
- **In-group collectivism** refers to the degree to which people express pride, loyalty, and cohesiveness in their groups or families.
- **Gender egalitarianism** measures the degree to which a cultural group minimizes gender role differences and promotes gender equality.
- **Assertiveness** refers to the degree to which people in a culture are determined, assertive, confrontational, and aggressive in their social relationships.

- **Future orientation** refers to the extent to which people engage in future-oriented behaviors such as planning, investing, and delaying gratification.
- **Performance orientation** describes the extent to which a cultural group encourages and rewards its members for improved performance and excellence.
- **Humane orientation** refers to the degree to which a culture encourages and rewards people for being fair, altruistic, generous, and caring to others.

The United States falls into the Anglo cluster, which also includes Canada, Australia, Ireland, England, South African whites, and New Zealand. These countries are high in performance orientation and low in in-group collectivism. This means that people in these countries tend to be competitive, results oriented, and less attached to their families and other groups as those in other countries. The other nine regional clusters identified by the GLOBE studies are Confucian Asia, Eastern Europe, Germanic Europe, Latin America, Latin Europe, Middle East, Nordic Europe, Southern Asia, and Sub-Saharan Africa. Table 5.3 provides a classification of the cultural clusters with regard to how they scored on each cultural dimension.

Although the GLOBE study has generated a great deal of data from many sources, it has received some criticism. It does not provide a clear set of assumptions or propositions that form a single theory about the way that culture relates to leadership. It also measures a broad variety of characteristics that are difficult to identify as a set of universal attributes in isolation from the context in which they occur. As should be now

Opportunity to Reflect

Identify your own individual style based on the description of cultural dimensions provided above. How representative is your personal assessment in relation to your cultural group? Are you a good example of your cultural classification? If not, identify what makes you different. How did your life, professional experiences, memberships, and professional affiliations change your cultural value orientations?

Table 5.3 Cultural clusters classified on cultural dimensions

Cultural dimension	High-score clusters	Low-score clusters
Assertiveness Orientation	Eastern Europe	Nordic Europe
Future Orientation	Germanic Europe	Eastern Europe
Gender Egalitarianism	Germanic Europe	Latin America
Humane Orientation	Nordic Europe	Middle East
In-group Collectivism	Eastern Europe	Middle East
Institutional Collectivism	Nordic Europe	Germanic Europe
Performance Orientation	Southern Asia	Latin Europe
Power Distance	Sub-Saharan Africa	Anglo
Uncertainty Avoidance	Confucian Asia	Germanic Europe
	Eastern Europe	Nordic Europe
	Latin America	Germanic Europe
	Middle East	Latin America
	Southern Asia	Latin Europe
	Nordic Europe	Eastern Europe
	Confucian Asia	Latin America
	Anglo	Nordic Europe
	Confucian Asia	Eastern Europe
	Germanic Europe	Latin America
	No clusters	Middle East
	Germanic Europe	
	Nordic Europe	

Source: Adapted from House, Hanges, Javidan, Dorfman, and Gupta (2004).

clearly understood, one of the key differences in a discourse approach to leadership and that of more traditional approaches is the importance of the context of the communication event regarding its effect on the emergence of the actual interaction.

Studies of Cultural Leadership Styles

The focus on identifying particular leadership characteristics and cultural preferences for the use of these characteristics has led researchers to try to identify preferences for leadership styles. Most of this work has been conducted by management scholars using survey research techniques.

Paternalistic Leadership

Paternalistic leadership "combines strong discipline and authority with fatherly benevolence and moral integrity couched in a 'personalistic' atmosphere."[8] Paternalistic leadership is composed of three main elements: authoritarianism, benevolence, and moral leadership.[9] At its roots, paternalistic leadership refers to a hierarchical relationship in which the leader takes personal interest in the workers' professional and personal lives in a manner resembling a parent, and expects loyalty and respect in return.[10]

A great deal of research has been conducted on the prevalence of paternalistic leadership style in non-Western business organizations, which tend to be situated in collectivist cultures. Studies have shown the prevalence of paternalistic leadership in countries, such as China and Taiwan.[11] For example, Hui and Tan reported results of a small body of research on Chinese leadership, which rather randomly mixed supervisory and leadership processes.[12] They found that Chinese employees want their leaders to be considerate and benevolent, adhere to the Confucian parental role, and exercise sound moral judgment, such as being self-restrained, honest toward fellow colleagues and subordinates, trustworthy, and impartial. Sarros and Santora surveyed 181 executives of Australia, Japan, China, and Russia to explore the linkage between their value orientations and leadership behaviors. They found that Chinese executives emphasized values such as benevolence, harmony with others, and self-restraint.[13] They also noted that compared to executives from the other three countries, Chinese executives did not identify independent thinking as a key value dimension.

Considerably less research has been done, however, on whether paternalistic leadership exists in Western cultures. Recently, there has been an increase in interest in studying paternalistic leadership in non-Western cultures. Although it is a relatively new area of focus in leadership research, some evidence has supported the relationship between paternalism and positive work attitudes in numerous cultures, including the Middle East, Latin America, and Pacific Asia.[14] Pellegrini, Scandura, and Jayaraman examined paternalism in the Western business context and found that paternalistic leadership was positively associated with job satisfaction in India, but not in the United States. In both Indian and United States cultures, paternalistic leadership was positively related to leader-member exchange and organizational commitment.[15] (The leader-member exchange theory of leadership focuses on the two-way relationship between supervisors and subordinates. The theory assumes that leaders develop an exchange with each of their subordinates, and that the quality of these leader-member exchange (LMX) relationships influences subordinates' responsibility, decision influence, access to resources, and performance.[16])

Transformational and Transactional Leadership

In addition to paternalistic leadership, other leadership styles that have been studied include those emanating from the transactional and transformational leadership theories discussed in Chapters 1 and 4. If you recall, transactional leadership is characterized by a give-and-take relationship using rewards as an incentive, while transformational leadership is loosely defined as a charismatic leadership style that rallies subordinates around a common goal with enthusiasm and support. These concepts were introduced by Bass and have been studied throughout the years, resulting in claims that these types of leadership styles are transferable across cultures. In fact, Bass and Avolio went as far as to give an optimal leadership profile for leaders around the world.[17]

Shahin and Wright[18] decided to test this theory in Egypt, an emerging market that had yet to be studied. In a questionnaire study of employees at 10 banks, results indicated that only 3 of the 7 factors that were found in the ideal leadership style in Egypt corresponded with the U.S. factors. The other four were unique to Egypt or perhaps the Middle East in general. These results indicate an inability to assume that transactional and transformational leadership will necessarily succeed in non-Western cultures. Casimir, Waldman, Bartram, and Yang[19] similarly found that these leadership styles may not be as universal as some assume. In a study of transactional and transformational leadership in China and Australia, results indicated that transformational leadership significantly predicted performance and trust in the Australian population, while only predicting trust, and not performance in the Chinese population. Transactional leadership did not predict trust or performance in either population. As a result of these and similar studies, some researchers have suggested that it is unwise to take leadership models developed in the West and attempt to apply them in non-Western cultures.

Opportunity to Reflect

Think about your experiences with people in different leadership positions. Can you identify their leadership styles? How successful were they in leading others? Can you identify any correlations between the culture of the organization, the values and practices of the leader and employees, and the leadership style?

A Discursive Approach to Leadership Style in Cross-Cultural Teams

We have taken a different approach in our own studies of interactions among decision-making teams composed of participants from both individualistic and collectivist cultures. Rather than testing whether a particular style of leadership as developed by traditional leadership models works well within these multicultural teams, we have used discursive methods to first identify the type of leadership that is used (see Chapter 3) and then survey the participants to assess their degree of satisfaction with the leadership style used in decision-making meetings.

We first developed a rubric to assess communication-based leadership attribute preferences. The rubric was based on the six global leader behaviors identified by the GLOBE Research Program. Twenty six participants from five different countries, United States, Korea, China, Japan, and Taiwan, participated in a simulated decision-making activity. At the end of the activity, all participants were asked to complete a questionnaire that included a discursive measure of leadership attributes.

The analysis of the communication-based measure to identify leadership styles using the survey mechanism revealed the following results (see Table 5.4).

Of the five styles, the preferences for being "decisive and task oriented" and "involving others in decision-making process" were displayed across all cultural groups; however, the differences emerged across cultures in the predominant features of "doing leadership." Whereas the U.S. team members identified "decisive and task oriented" as the most important characteristic of a leader, the other cultures listed it as second in importance. Japanese valued modesty, compassion, and support over

Table 5.4 Cross-cultural comparison of communication-based leadership styles

	First choice	Second choice	Third choice
United States	Decisive and task oriented	Involved others in decision-making process	Modest, compassionate, and supportive
China	Status-conscious and procedural	Involved others in decision-making process and Decisive and task oriented (tie)	
Korea	Involved others in decision-making process	Decisive and task oriented	Status-conscious and procedural
Japan	Modest, compassionate, and supportive	Involved others in decision-making process and Decisive and task oriented (tie)	

being decisive and task oriented, Koreans identified "involving others in decision-making process" feature as the most important attribute of a leader, and the Chinese valued the "status conscious and procedural" style the most.

Language Proficiency in Cross-Cultural Teams

Some studies have documented that the lack of language proficiency impedes the effectiveness of communication in international settings. Du-Babcock, for example, found that Cantonese students were less effective in group decision making when speaking English than when they spoke their native language, which indicates that language proficiency may affect group outcomes.[20] Clyne noted that in English-speaking situations, international participants are disadvantaged because they are being judged by native speakers who are operating within their own cultural norms based on their cultural values systems.[21] In her analysis of American and Japanese business discourse, Yamada discusses negative attitudes that are formed about a cultural group that does not emulate native-like language competencies.[22] Even though Clyne recognized that international participants in an English-speaking situation may be at a disadvantage, he found that language proficiency does not have a significant effect on group success. Our own work in this area, however, found that language proficiency *per se* did not affect the contribution and participation rates of those from East Asian cultures in group decision-making meetings using English.[23]

Other approaches to the language issue in multicultural settings include an argument for the development and use of a Business English Lingua Franca (BELF) owned by the international business discourse community with emphasis on achieving a communicative goal rather than native speaker-like language proficiency. The argument hinges on the fact that, at present, English is the *de facto* language of many intercultural business transactions. Proponents of the BELF approach, argue that rather than expecting participants to use native speaker-like language proficiency, a model should be developed based on a set of norms determined within the cultural context of the communication.

In this study, our data set consisted of transcripts of video-recordings of simulated small-group decision-making meetings conducted in English. Eighty four individuals who were native speakers of East Asian languages and English were chosen to participate in the simulation. Our East Asian participants were primarily from Japan, China, and Korea. Participants were put into small groups composed of different types of members; homogeneous groups composed of native speakers of East Asian languages and homogeneous groups composed of native speakers of American English were compared with heterogeneous groups composed of both native speakers of East Asian languages and native speakers of American English.

To measure communicative performance, we used a discourse-based approach and developed a mechanism to track member interaction by six identifiable variables. In order to measure member contribution, we tracked the number of turns taken by participants, the number of words spoken, and the average turn length. We measured member participation by looking at turn-taking strategies, that is, overlaps, backchannels, and latching. (These elements of discourse were explained in Chapter 2.)

Table 5.5 shows a comparison between native speakers of East Asian languages and native speakers of American English working in

Table 5.5 A comparison of Americans and East Asians in
homogeneous groups T(p)

Category Variable	T(p)	Mean of midranks (Americans)	Mean of midranks (Asians)	Difference of midranks**	SE of mean of midranks
Turns	0.62 (0.541)	16.13	18.35	−2.22	3.58
Words	0.75 (0.46)	18.08	15.35	2.73	3.62
Turn length	−7.221 (0.000)	22.3	8.85	13.45	1.86*
Overlaps	−0.80 (0.43)	18.05	15.38	2.67	3.35
Backchannels	−0.07 (0.95)	17.1	16.85	0.25	3.71
Latching	5.01 (0.000)	12.4	24.08	−11.68	2.33*

$*p < .05$
** The main entry reports the difference of midranks that was used test the hypothesis that all J independent groups have identical distributions. Standard errors are provided in a separate column.

Note: T(p) = length of turn, SE = standard error.

homogeneous groups in each of the six areas that we analyzed. The first three variables in the table indicate the degree of contribution measured by the number of turns, number of words, and turn length, while the last three variables indicate the level of participation measured by overlaps, backchannels, and latching.

The comparison between homogeneous teams composed of native English speakers and speakers of East Asian languages did not produce statistically significant results, except in two areas. As shown in Table 5.5, when working in homogeneous teams, speakers of East Asian languages and native speakers of English did not show significant differences in the degree of contribution; their turn taking and amount of speaking were not significantly different, although speakers of East Asian languages took shorter turns ($p = 0.000$) than native speakers of English. However, the shorter turn length did not affect the overall rate of contribution: East Asian speakers working in homogeneous groups took as many turns and spoke as many words as U.S.-born students in homogeneous groups. Such a finding indicates that there were no significant differences in the degree of contribution of speakers of East Asian languages and U.S.-born speakers of English when working in homogeneous groups and speaking English.

Both groups also demonstrated similar patterns of participation measured by looking at overlaps and backchannels. The only area that showed significant differences between the two groups was latching. Speakers of East Asian languages in homogeneous groups were using latching, changing turns without a perceptible pause, more frequently than U.S.-born speakers of English ($p = 0.000$). (Latching is discussed in more detail below.)

These findings demonstrate that in fact the degree of contribution and participation between homogenous U.S.-born teams and homogeneous teams comprised of native speakers of East Asian languages is quite similar when using English. Our analysis suggests that when placed in homogeneous teams, East Asian speakers with English as a second-language proficiency demonstrate participation patterns that are very similar to those exhibited by native speakers of English.

However, this pattern did not manifest in the mixed or heterogeneous teams. Table 5.6 shows a comparison between native speakers of American English and native speakers of East Asian languages in homogeneous and heterogeneous teams (the first three variables in the table mark the degree of contribution, while the last three indicate the level of participation).

The results show that there were significant differences between the two groups in almost all areas of analysis. Native speakers of English showed significantly higher levels of contribution, they took more turns ($p = 0.000$), produced more words ($p = 0.000$) and their turns were longer ($p = 0.011$). In addition, their participation was also significantly higher compared to native speakers of East Asian languages in all areas, except for latching. They overlapped more frequently ($p = 0.000$) and used more backchannels ($p = 0.000$). These findings confirm that in heterogeneous groups, native speakers of English dominate the discussion by saying more, speaking more frequently, and taking longer turns. They are also "louder" and more involved, since overlapping is associated with a more aggressive, "high involvement" style. This style may be considered pushy, aggressive, or fast-talking by other cultural groups.[24] They were more vocal in reacting to other members' contribution by backchanneling

Table 5.6 A comparison of Americans and East Asians in heterogeneous groups T(p)

Category					
Variable	T(p)	Mean of midranks (Americans)	Mean of midranks (Asians)	Difference of midranks**	SE of mean of midranks
Turns	.577 (0.000)	33.78	14.88	18.9	2.49*
Words	−9.10 (0.000)	34.37	14.05	20.32	2.23*
Turn length	−2.73 (0.011)	30.63	19.38	11.25	4.13*
Overlaps	−4.72 (0.000)	32.62	16.55	16.07	3.4*
Backchannels	−2.72 (0.01)	30.55	19.5	11.05	4.06*
Latching	−1.06 (0.30)	27.88	23.31	4.57	4.33

*$p < .05$
** The main entry reports the difference of midranks that was used test the hypothesis that all J independent groups have identical distributions. Standard errors are provided in a separate column.

Note: T(p) = length of turn, SE = standard error.

more frequently. The only area that did not produce significant difference was latching.

When placed in heterogeneous teams, native speakers of East Asian languages showed significantly lower contribution and participation patterns than their American counterparts. Because of their high English language proficiency and similar performance to U.S.-born students in homogenous teams, language proficiency alone cannot explain the lower rates of participation and contribution by speakers of East Asian languages in mixed teams. Consequently, other factors must account for these differences in heterogeneous groups.

Whereas our analysis of heterogeneous groups showed significant differences in contribution and participation rates between native speakers of American English and speakers of East Asian languages, one important finding of this study was that there were no significant differences in elements of discourse used by the two cultural groups when working in homogeneous groups. The homogeneous East Asian groups were comparable to U.S-born participants in both the degree of contribution and participation as measured by the six discourse elements tracked in our study. The only perceptible difference was in the area of contribution when speakers of East Asian languages took significantly shorter turns than native speakers of English. This finding is consistent with Clyne's research,[25] who observed cultural differences in turn length, with East Asians producing shorter turns.

The patterns of participation, again, produced very similar results for speakers of East Asian languages and native speakers of American English when working in homogeneous groups. The only significant difference was noted in the area of latching, where East Asian speakers latched more than their U.S.-born counterparts.

It is interesting to note that in heterogeneous groups these patterns were reversed, and native speakers of English latched significantly more than speakers of East Asian languages. This reverse effect prompted us to look more closely at the way the two cultural groups used latching. What we found was that the function of latching is different between these two cultural groups. Native speakers of English used latching as a way of introducing a new topic, taking the floor, or advancing the decision-making process by offering new information as is shown in the example below from a group of native speakers of English working in a homogeneous group ("z" indicates an instance of latching):

Speaker 1:	Um, so I'll say that that our sales team has come up with a letter to present to those professors-
Speaker 2:	z I'd like to intro[duce you guys to our sales group
Speaker 1:	[to] z right-
Speaker 2:	Hi, my name is blah [blah] blah blah,
Speaker 1:	[right] z then say that we've come up with this letter to present to the university professors in the, in China, hopefully convincing them that the use of our, what's the name of our product? Our-
Speaker 3:	3G.

In this brief exchange, both Speaker 1 and Speaker 2 use latching. The first instance of latching occurs when Speaker 2 offers new information by volunteering to introduce his team; Speaker 1 then accepts his offer by latching with a short "right" trying to gain the floor again. However, his first attempt is not successful until the second instance of latching when he offers new information in planning the presentation of their product.

East Asian speakers, on the other hand, used latching quite differently. Their use of latching was mostly cooperative, and in many cases they were finishing each others' sentences or offering support to the previous speakers. The example below is taken from an exchange of East Asian speakers working in homogeneous teams:

Speaker 1:	I think we're going to first find the target market, actually not the whole China.
Speaker 2:	Mm-hmmm.
Speaker 1:	But probably like
Speaker 3:	z the younger group. More trendy group.
Speaker 1:	yeah.

In this example, Speaker 3 uses latching to finish Speaker's 1 turn, which Speaker 1 then acknowledges by backchanneling "yeah."

Another example of latching use by East Asian speakers working in homogeneous teams follows:

Speaker 1:	We can have the Song Girls
Speaker 2:	zThe Song Girls are all holding it in their hands. How funny would that be!

In this example, Speaker 2 picks up Speaker's 1 idea of using Song Girls to market the product and develops it further by offering additional details.

Based on this analysis, there seems to be a fundamental difference in the way latching is used by native speakers of English and speakers of East Asian languages in decision-making meetings held in English. Our data shows that whereas English speakers use latching to offer an entirely new propositional content, speakers of East Asian languages build and extend on the proposition offered by the previous speaker. These differences seem to suggest different conversational patterns, one being more competitive and individualistic and the latter being more collaborative and supportive. This difference may explain some of the changes that we saw when the East Asian speakers were moved from homogeneous to mixed groups.

A second factor that may explain this change in participation and contribution rates among our East Asian participants when working in mixed teams might be explained by the issue of face. As mentioned earlier, Clyne[26] and Charles[27] have brought up the disadvantage non-native speakers of English face when they operate in the *lingua franca* of the business domain (i.e., English) but are being judged by native speakers of English according to the latter's cultural norms. According to Charles, "language is a very personal thing. If people, on a daily basis, face situations where they feel deprived of their ability to communicate and express themselves adequately, there is [...] a sense of frustration, and a struggle to maintain dignity."[28] As was discussed in Chapter 4, maintaining dignity is an essential element of the construct of face.

Opportunity to Reflect

Think about your own experiences working in multicultural groups. Do people from different cultures participate and contribute to the discussion equally? What are some of the differences that you can identify and what effect they have had on the group as a whole?

Effects of Leadership Style

As was discussed in Chapter 3, our research also has led us to identify three styles of leadership: directive, cooperative, and collaborative. A review of the elements of those styles is provided in Table 5.7.

We have analyzed how these styles of leadership affect the contribution and participation rates of East Asian participants working in groups with U.S. Americans. We have also collected survey data from research participants to measure their attitudes about the group experience in two areas, their satisfaction with the group decision-making process and their perceived sense of inclusion and being valued in the process.

Table 5.7 A summary of the differences and similarities exhibited in discourse styles by leadership types

Discourse elements	Directive leader	Cooperative leader	Collaborative leader
Meaning of questions	To direct members	To solicit participation	To frame the interaction and check for agreement
Links between turns	Few	To acknowledge contribution	Some acknowledgement of contribution
Topic shifts	Abrupt	Smooth	Smooth
Listening	Minimal	Active	Minimal
Simultaneous speech	Interruptions	Few overlaps	Frequent cooperative overlaps

The findings from our survey indicated that U.S.-born participants and East Asian participants did not produce statistically significant differences in responses to questions designed to measure their overall satisfaction with the group decision-making process. However, in response to questions designed to measure their perceived sense of inclusion and being valued in the process, East Asian language speakers reported that they did not feel as included, valued, or supported as their American counterparts.

The disparity in responses about inclusion given by U.S. participants and those from the East Asian countries led us to look at the style of leadership that was emerging in the groups. In the discussion that follows, we draw upon the same two cases that were the focus of discussion in Chapter 3. In the first case, the leader used the Directive Style while in the second case, the leader used the Cooperative Style.

Table 5.8 shows the actual counts of the average number of turns, words spoken, and words per turn for each cultural group.

In case study 1, the leader used a Directive Leadership Style. This style was more aggressive in that the leader used questions to direct members to select the leader's preferred choices, interrupted others, shifted topics abruptly back to his preferred topic, and minimal active listening techniques were used. In this context, on average, Americans took five times as many turns than Asian speakers (151 compared to 39) and produced 1170 words compared to 127. The difference in average turn length was

Table 5.8 Contribution to decision-making meetings by cultural group, case study 1

Cultural group	Average number of turns	Average number of words	Average words per turn
Asian speakers	39	127.5	3.2
American speakers	151	1170	7.7

Table 5.9 Contribution to decision-making meetings by cultural group, case study 2

Cultural group	Average number of turns	Average number of words	Average words per turn
Asian speakers	105.7	843.7	4.6
American speakers	152.5	870.5	5.7

also significantly longer, 7.7 words for Americans compared to 3.2 words for Asians.

In case study 2, in which a cooperative style of leadership is used, we see a different result as is shown in Table 5.9.

The results in Table 5.9 show a much more balanced interaction between the two cultural groups involved in case study 2. The Cooperative Leadership Style demonstrated by a female native speaker of English that included overt invitations of contribution resulted in a more inclusive leadership style that ensured a more collaborative decision-making process. The invitation to speak was expressed by frequent use of yes/no and open-ended questions to help ensure that all members of the group had a chance to express their opinion before reaching a group decision. Consensus was thus this group's preferred decision-making schema.

In this setting, the average contribution by American speakers was more similar to the average contribution of Asian speakers when compared to the results in case study 1. American speakers took 152 turns compared to 105 turns by Asian speakers. The average number of words spoken by American and Asian speakers was similar, 870 and 843, respectively. American speakers' turn length was longer than Asian speakers—5.7 compared to 4.6—but not nearly as different as in case study 1. This finding is consistent with Clyne,[29] who observed cultural differences in turn length, with East Asians producing shorter turns. Overall, member contribution was more balanced and more comparable across cultural groups in case study 2 as compared with case study 1.

No interaction analysis was completed for this third case study discussed in Chapter 3 in which a Collaborative Leadership Style emerged. That was because this leadership style was observed only in homogeneous American groups, that is, no mixed group composed of participants from both the U.S. or East Asian cultures demonstrated this particular leadership style.

Our study indicates that differing styles of leadership can affect the participation and contribution of members from different cultures when interacting in cross-cultural teams and may affect their feelings of inclusion within the group. It also provides some evidence that particular styles of and approaches to leadership may not be as successful with all cultural groups. For example, the notion of the strong, charismatic leader that emerges from some traditional approaches to leadership, that is, trait, transformational, and neocharismatic theories, may not be as successful in terms of participation and feelings of inclusion by group members of particular cultural backgrounds. Similarly, the more "free for all" approach of the Collaborative Leadership Style may not emerge in all cultures because of differences in cultural values or styles of communication. For example, differences in power distance, or the degree to which members of a cultural group expect and agree to how power should be shared, may affect whether participants feel comfortable interacting within a nonhierarchical structure. Power distance may partially explain why Asian participants who come from high-power cultures may not engage in the distributed leadership approach because of an expectation for a designated leader.

These findings may explain why the collaborative style of leadership generated more balanced participation and contribution among East Asian participants, since it might better reflect the values of being considerate and respectful of others. In contrast, the directive style might be seen as too aggressive and, given the fact that language proficiency may be another obstacle to equal participation in decision making, this style deters Asian participants from being equal partners in decision-making.

The distributed leadership approach similarly requires a more assertive style of communication to self-nominate to take the floor.

Identifying particular discourse practices can provide a more concrete way of looking at the enactment of leadership and enabling potential leaders to consciously approach the task with their audience in mind. For example, the specific discursive strategies as exhibited by Speaker 1 in case study 2 may create a more inclusive discussion space that can potentially produce more collaborative solutions and decisions while at the same time engaging participants from collectivist cultures in decision-making processes. Similarly, a more directive leadership style may not be the best approach when working with people from collectivist cultures if the goal is to encourage participation in and satisfaction with the group process among East Asian speakers.

Opportunity to Reflect

Can you identify your own preferred leadership style based on the classification provided above? If you were a participant in a meeting, which style would you prefer your leader to exhibit? Why?

Summary

Culture has an important effect on communication practices. **Culture** is defined as the learned set of beliefs, values, rules, norms, symbols, and traditions that are common to a group of people. It is a way of life, customs, and script for a group of people. Culture is a social construction.

Perhaps the most referenced study of culture is the research of Geert Hofstede, which identified five major dimensions on which cultures differ: power distance, uncertainty avoidance, individualism collectivism, masculinity–femininity, and long-term versus short-term orientation.

The Global Leadership and Organizational Behavior Effectiveness (GLOBE) research program incorporated Hofstede's cultural dimensions and Implicit Leadership Theory (ITL) into one study designed to measure whether certain leadership styles translate across cultures. The ILT asserts that people's underlying assumptions, stereotypes, beliefs, and schemas influence the extent to which they view someone as a good leader. The

GLOBE researchers divided the data from 62 countries into 10 regional clusters and identified nine cultural dimensions: uncertainty avoidance, power distance, institutional collectivism, in-group collectivism, gender egalitarianism, assertiveness, future orientation, performance orientation, and humane orientation.

The focus on identifying particular leadership characteristics and any cultural preferences for the use of these characteristics has led researchers to try to identify preferences for leadership styles. Paternalistic leadership combines strong discipline and authority with fatherly benevolence and moral integrity couched in a "personalistic" atmosphere. Paternalistic leadership is composed of three main elements: authoritarianism, benevolence, and moral leadership. Research conducted on the prevalence of this leadership style in non-Western business organizations, which tend to be situated in collectivist cultures, reveals a prevalence of paternalistic leadership in countries such as China and Taiwan.

In addition to paternalistic leadership, other leadership styles that have been studied include those emanating from the transactional and transformational leadership theories. Transactional leadership is characterized by a give-and-take relationship using rewards as an incentive, while transformational leadership is loosely defined as a charismatic leadership style that rallies subordinates around a common goal with enthusiasm and support. These concepts have been studied throughout the years, resulting in claims that these types of leadership styles are transferable across cultures. However, others studies have failed to substantiate this finding. Some researchers have suggested that it is unwise to take leadership models developed in the West and attempt to apply them in non-Western cultures.

Our own studies of leadership in the United States involving participants from East Asian countries found that being "decisive and task oriented" and "involving others in decision-making process" were displayed across all cultural groups; however, the differences emerged across cultures in the predominant features of "doing leadership." Whereas U.S. team members identified "decisive and task oriented" as the most important characteristic of a leader, the other cultures listed it as second in importance. Japanese valued modesty, compassion, and support over being decisive and task oriented, Koreans identified "involving others in decision-making process" feature as the most important attribute of a leader, and the Chinese most valued the "status conscious and procedural" style.

Our work has shown that language proficiency *per se* does not affect the contribution and participation rates of those from East Asian cultures in group decision-making meetings using English. Our analysis suggests that when placed in homogeneous teams, East Asian speakers with English as a second-language proficiency demonstrate participation patterns that are very similar to those exhibited by native speakers of English. However, this pattern did not manifest in mixed or heterogeneous teams. When placed in heterogeneous teams, native speakers of East Asian languages showed significantly lower contribution and participation patterns than their American counterparts.

We have analyzed how the Directive and Cooperative Leadership styles affect the contribution and participation rates of East Asian participants working in groups with Americans. In teams where the leader displayed a Directive Leadership style, Americans on average took 5 times as many turns than Asian speakers and produced nearly 10 times the number of words. Average turn length was nearly twice the number of words for Americans. In contrast, in a team where the leader displayed the Cooperative Leadership style, the average contribution by American speakers was more similar to the average contribution of Asian speakers as was the average number of words spoken by American and Asian speakers. American speakers' turn length was longer than Asian speakers—5.7 compared to 4.6—but not nearly as different as in the team with a directive leader.

CHAPTER 6

Gender and Leadership

There is no either/or between being competitive and collaborative. You have to be both and decide which in each situation.

—Cathie Black, Former Chairman and President,

Hearst Magazines

The first thing that should be understood when we talk about gender is that it is a social construct, just as is ethnicity or cultural difference. Gender is different from biological sex. It is a social patterning that has been created over time and has been passed down from generation to generation within a culture. It is a learned behavior that we enact each day to "create" our gendered selves. We do so through our clothing and accessory choices, our mannerisms, our vocal qualities, the way we walk and talk, and the things we say and do.

It can be difficult to see this fact when one is completely immersed in a particular culture, but our assumptions about what is "male" or "female" in terms of cultural display and enactment could be otherwise and often are in reality. That is, traditional ideas such as "men should wear the pants in the family"—a notion that is still held by many in the United States today—have come up against such realities as the fact that 40% of households with children have single parents and of those, 63% are mothers.[1] In these relational units, the so-called men or heads of household are often wearing skirts (or at least find it socially acceptable to do so!). Such paradoxes that arise between cultural values and reality demonstrate that gender is a social construct that "sticks" even though associated facts may no longer support the assumptions generally related to that construct.

This problem arises in the workplace, too, and affects one's ability to be perceived as a leader. Since women are the most negatively affected by gender constructs, or stereotypes, in the workplace and because more research has been done on women, the discussion here will be pursued from their perspective. This exploration is also useful to men, however, since, as leaders, reflecting on our responses in similar situations can help us to understand our own gendered behaviors and interact more effectively with others.

The issue of what has been called "the double bind," will be the first explored in this chapter. This discussion will be followed by an explanation of the features of gendered talk and ways of talking that trouble the double bind.

The "Double Bind"

A three-part research series on stereotyping sponsored by IBM found that managers perceived distinct differences between women and men leaders.[2] The respondents in the study were senior U.S. managers, more than 30% of whom were CEOs. They perceived that more women leaders than men leaders were effective at "caretaker" behaviors, such as supporting others and rewarding subordinates. In contrast, they perceived that more men leaders than women leaders were effective at "take charge" behaviors, such as delegating and problem solving. Notably, the study finds these perceptions are not supported by research on actual leadership behavior, which indicates that gender is not a reliable predictor of how a person will lead.

These perceptions hold not only in the United States but also among Western European managers. A follow-up study looked at perceptions of women's and men's leadership and compared managers' perceptions from four groups of culturally similar countries—Anglo (United Kingdom, United States), Germanic (the Netherlands, Germany), Latin (France, Italy, Spain), and Nordic (Denmark, Norway, Sweden)—and found that in every group, managers held stereotypic perceptions of women's and men's leadership. Further, the findings suggested that these perceptions bear some striking similarities across cultures. Importantly, in some cultures, stereotypic perceptions discredited the effectiveness of women leaders as without highly valued leadership attributes.

A third stage of the study showed how common perceptions can create difficult predicaments for women leaders. The findings strongly suggested that, on account of stereotypes, women's leadership talent is routinely underestimated and underutilized in organizations—even though organizations need women's talent in order to succeed. Although women constitute almost half of the U.S. workforce and hold more than 50% of management and professional positions, they make up only 2% of Fortune 500 CEOs. The underrepresentation of women at the top occurs across occupations and industries and regardless of how many women occupy management positions within the organization. A growing body of research points to stereotyping as one of the key contributors to this gender gap in corporate leadership.[3]

Essentially, because of these stereotypes, women who wish to be seen as leaders face a double bind: if they act like women are supposed to, they are seen as weak. If they take on the attributes associated with men, then they are seen as too aggressive. Neither is a good alternative and hence, the name "double bind": a situation in which a person—in this case, a woman—must choose between equally unsatisfactory alternatives; a punishing and inescapable dilemma.[4]

According to the Catalyst study conducted by the leading nonprofit organization with a mission to expand opportunities for women and business, women leaders face three particular dilemmas:

- **Extreme perceptions: Too soft, too tough, and never just right.** When women leaders act in ways that are consistent with gender stereotypes (i.e., focus on work relationships and express concern for other people's perspectives), they are viewed as less competent leaders, as being too soft. When women act in ways that are inconsistent with such stereotypes, however (i.e., act assertively, focus on work task, display ambition), their behavior is judged as too tough, even unfeminine.[5]
- **The High competence threshold: Women leaders face higher standards and lower rewards than men leaders.** When it comes to proving leadership capabilities, women are subjected to higher standards than are men. They have to work harder to show the same level of competence and have to confront additional trade-offs than their male counterparts in order to lead effectively. Sheryl Sandberg, chief operating

officer of Facebook, puts it in perspective when she stated that men are promoted based on potential while women are promoted based on past accomplishments.[6]

- **Competent but disliked: Women leaders are perceived as competent or likable but rarely both.** Women who adopt a "masculine" leadership style are viewed more negatively. Although they might be viewed as competent because of their leadership style, they also receive more negative evaluations of their interpersonal skills than women who adopt a "feminine" style.[7] Hence, even acting in counter-stereotypical ways has potential harmful consequences for women leaders and may negatively impact their work relationships and access to social networks.

Gender stereotypes can also create problems for men. Inherent in gender stereotypes is the assumption that masculine and feminine characteristics (including "taking-care" and "taking-charge" behaviors) are mutually exclusive. While these perceptions target the "outsiders"—women leaders—to a larger extent than they do men leaders, they in fact affect all leaders. By creating a false dichotomy between women's and men's characteristics, stereotypes place both women and men leaders in relatively narrow categories of style and behaviors while limiting the range of effective behaviors within the workplace overall.

As these studies suggest, gender stereotypes create challenges to both men and women who aspire to be leaders. The next section will discuss features of gendered talk.

Opportunity to Reflect

Do you agree with the findings of the Catalyst study regarding the dilemmas women face in the workplace? Why or why not?

Features of Gendered Talk

Dozens of research studies have identified elements of gendered talk as shown in Table 6.1. Feminine interactional styles tend to be facilitative,

Table 6.1 Widely cited characteristics of "feminine" and "masculine" styles

Feminine	Masculine
Indirect	Direct
Conciliatory	Confrontational
Facilitative	Competitive
Collaborative	Autonomous
Minor contribution (in public)	Dominates speaking time publicly
Supportive feedback	Aggressive interruptions
Person/process-oriented	Task/outcome-oriented
Affectively oriented	Referentially oriented

Source: Holmes and Stubbe (2003). p. 574.

supportive, conciliatory, indirect, collaborative, publicly modest, and affectively oriented. Masculine interactional styles, on the other hand, tend to be competitive, aggressive interrupting, confrontational, direct, autonomous, publicly dominating, and task oriented.

An abbreviated overview of the pertinent research will be presented here to illustrate how femininity and masculinity are enacted through talk. It should be noted that stereotypical speech can be used by both genders, with oftentimes different effects.

Use of Latching, Overlaps, Hedges, and Questions

We will begin with a discussion of some of Jennifer Coates's work that we have already referred to in Chapters 2 and 3. In her studies of men and women in conversation or what she calls "friendly talk," Coates found that women tend to construct talk jointly and that the group takes priority over the individual as the women's voices combine to construct a shared text.[8] Utterances are often jointly constructed; in other words, speakers often co-operate to produce a chunk of talk. For example, in one of the conversations she collected, the following utterance, "I'm sure he's not/peeping," was produced by two friends, the second speaker adding the last word to complete the chunk.[9] (This is an example of *latching*, which was discussed in Chapter 3.) Jointly constructed utterances may involve more than just the final word, as in the following example: "They said they kept bumping into all sorts of people/ that they knew," where the second speaker adds the clause "that they knew."[10]

In addition, Coates observed that women friends often combine as speakers so that two or more voices may contribute to talk at the same time. This kind of overlapping speech is not seen as competitive, as a way of grabbing a turn, because the various contributions to talk are on the same theme. For example, in a conversation about looking after elderly parents, one woman in Coates' study said, "all of a sudden the roles are all reversed," while at the same time her friend said, "you become a parent, yeah."[11]

Women's friendly talk is also characterized by the sensitive use of hedges (words and phrases like "maybe," "sort of," "I mean"), which dampen the force of controversial utterances and help preserve open discussion, and by the frequent use of questions whose main function is interactive rather than information-seeking (i.e., the question, "there are limits aren't there?," checks that a shared perspective obtains and does not expect an answer except perhaps for "yeah" or "mhm").[12]

While women's voices combine and overlap, men take turns to hold court. Male friends prefer a one-at-a-time pattern of talking, with one speaker holding the floor at any one time; overlapping speech is avoided. Men also hedge less, and they use questions to seek information from each other, taking it in turns to play the expert.[13]

These differences were observed by Coates in all-male and all-female talk. The women's talk involved discussion of highly personal issues, such as child abuse, feminine issues, and relationships, as well as talk about more general topics. The sharing of personal experiences was matched by the sharing of the conversational floor. Men, by contrast, seemed to prefer more impersonal topics (politics, beer-making, sound systems, for example), topics that allow participants to take turns at being the expert.[14] It should be noted that this data was collected in the context of friendship and that a business context may alter topic selection. Further, this data was collected from homogeneous groups of women and men, and the mixing of genders can create more complex outcomes.

Taking the Floor

Early discourse studies often used "turn" and "floor" interchangeably. More research, though, has shown that "taking the floor" is different than taking a turn in that the floor is "variously and indirectly defined as a speaker, a turn, and control over part of the conversation."[15] The notion of floor was developed more by Edelsky, who proposed that there are two types of floors, singly developed floors and collaborative floors.[16] This is an important distinction when we look at gendered talk.

In Edelsky's study, which involved recording five meetings of a standing faculty committee comprised of seven women and four men, she found that singly developed floors in which one person held control over part of the conversation, were more prevalent than collaborative ones. In most meetings, there were twice as many single floors, and each single-floor episode was considerably longer than the collaborative floor episodes. Subsequent research by Coates has shown that women are far more inclined to use the latter type of floor, and it can be stereotypically associated with a feminine interactional style.[17] The single, one-at-a-time floor can alternately be classified with a stereotypically masculine interactional style.[18]

Here is an example of single-floor holding from Edelsky's work. It shows how, even though another is taking turns in the conversation, the floor is still held by the main speaker, Manny:[19]

Manny:	. . . in racist comments he made in his hour commentary on [Sunday]
Rafe:	[Oh, he did?]
Manny:	about the game.
Rafe:	What were they?
Manny:	One was with reference to
	couldn't see him very well.

And here's an example of a collaboratively developed floor from the same study. This exchange is taking place within a meeting involving other participants:[20]

Mary:	(to Sally) (low voice) I wonder if we should talk to Martha and see
Sally:	(to Mary) (low voice) Is that his wife?
Marion:	(to Sally) (low voice) Yeah.
Mary:	(to Sally and Marion) (low voice) Shall I go call her?

In this exchange, no one person is controlling the conversation; it is being constructed collaboratively by those involved.

Overlaps

As was discussed earlier, cooperative overlaps, or "jointly constructed" utterances, can be viewed as supportive simultaneous talk and are thus characterized as stereotypically feminine. Supportive simultaneous talk can be seen as a strategy of politeness since it pays attention to the need to save the face of the other. It thus signals solidarity with the other.

In contrast, Holmes defined uncooperative overlap, or an interruption, as a "disruptive turn" and as stereotypically masculine, since it is considered impolite, or lacking a regard for the face of the other.[21] Interruptions can be identified as an attempt to change the topic or to cut someone off and take the floor, as shown below:

Lucy:	I think one of the solutions we should consider is to survey [employees]
John:	[We know] the best solution so let's just put it in place and stop wasting time.

Amount of Talk

The jury is still out on who talks the most in interactions, but most researchers agree it depends on the context of the discussion—where it is happening and why—and the social structure of the discussion. Most agree that men and women are acculturated to talk about different things in different settings. For example, women are expected to use talk to a greater extent than men to establish and maintain relationships and thus they talk to keep interaction flowing smoothly and to show goodwill toward others. They also talk about feelings and socioemotional matters relevant to interpersonal relationships to a greater extent than men.[22] This type of talk is more likely to happen in informal situations.

In more formal situations, the majority of studies find that men talk more than women. This outcome has been attributed to *status characteristics theory*, which focuses on how status differences organize interaction. According to this theory, individuals involved in social interactions evaluate themselves relative to the other individuals involved and come to hold expectations as to how and how well they will perform in relation to every other participant in the interaction. These "self-other performance expectations" provide the structure of the interaction, which then determines the subsequent interaction. A status characteristic is any characteristic that is socially valued and has differentially evaluated states. These include race, sex, gender, education, age, and organizational office. Research has shown that those with higher status participate more in task-oriented dyads or groups than those with lower status.[23] Since men have traditionally held higher status than have women, research would lead one to expect men to talk more in task-oriented or instrumental situations.

Use of Speech Acts

Holmes, Stubbe, and Vine have demonstrated the value of using speech acts to examine how power and authority are enacted in workplace interaction. The speech acts they define are as follows:

- Setting the agenda
- Summarizing progress
- Closing an interaction
- Issuing directives
- Expressing approval
- Issuing criticisms
- Issuing warnings
- Issuing challenges[24]

Setting the agenda, summarizing progress, and closing an interaction demonstrate how superiors control the structure and development of meetings, while the remaining functions reveal how managers actually manage and instruct their subordinates through the speech elements they use.[25]

Directives

Researchers have argued that women in positions of authority will be more likely to issue directives in a face-saving manner, by using such tactics as indirectness to avoid potentially confrontational reactions.[26] Other speech acts that can be seen as stereotypically feminine are mitigating directives, criticisms, warnings, and challenges.

Directives can be mitigated by taking the form of interrogatives—a sentence or an expression that asks a question—or declaratives—a statement in the form of a declaration.[27] Directives can also be mitigated by rationalizations and justifications, hesitations, and pauses. Hedging tactics can also be used to mitigate directives; these include the use of tag questions; modal verbs (*can/could, may/might, must, will/would,* and *shall/should*); lexical items, such as *perhaps* and *conceivable*; and pragmatic particles, such as *sort of* and *I think*.[28] In addition, the use of such words, such as *let's*, signals a proposal rather than a command and show deference to the other party, while the use of the collective pronoun "we" accompanied with "can" or "could" indicate possibility rather than necessity.[29]

> Gina: You just need to sort of sink yourselves in, and if you want information go to sort of the nearest person that's doing a regular search to trawl it for a little; go on there now.

In this example, Gina uses minimizers "just" and "sort of" as a hedge twice and a conditional "if" and "little" to mitigate her directive for members' computer training.[30]

In contrast, directives given without mitigation, may directly threaten or attack face, and can thus be viewed as stereotypically masculine. Mullany classified directives given without mitigation into two types: unmitigated and aggravated.[31] An unmitigated directive is an order or demand that is used by a person with legitimate power, while an aggravated directive is a demand that is considered impolite in that it may be seen as face threatening. This may come from the fact that the person giving the directive doesn't have legitimate power to do so.

In the following example, Gina gives an unmitigated directive using a stereotypically masculine style:

> Gina: Anything to do with scheduling issues, give it to Erin the next time.

The following example is of an aggravated directive given by Gina that threatens the face needs of Ann.

> Erin: We moved the empty boxes to the bathroom [and]
> Ann: [What about the]
> Gina: [Hold on a minute] wait till she's done
> Erin: The books have been moved to the back of the coffee room.

Gina's command for Ann to "hold on a minute" and "wait" draws upon a stereotypically masculine speech style to challenge Ann's interruption of Erin.

As was discussed in Chapters 1 and 3, those viewed as having "expert power," even though not in positions of authority, can also enact power by issuing directives, giving criticism, expressing approval, or even issuing warnings or challenges.

Expressing Approval

As expressions of approval are face-enhancing, they are generally considered as stereotypically feminine. In the formal context of business meetings, approval may be expressed by complimenting the skills and abilities of the recipient. Interestingly, when those of lower status express approval to supervisors, the supervisors tend to interpret such occasions as subordinates agreeing with them rather than giving a direct evaluation of the superior's performance. Of course, expressions of approval also may not be sincere, which may affect their reception.[32]

Criticism

Superiors are legitimately entitled to criticize their subordinates due to the institutional power they hold. However, criticism can be expressed in different ways. As with directives, it can be expressed in an unmitigated as well as an aggravated fashion.[33] Both of these methods are seen as stereotypically masculine, while criticisms that are mitigated may be seen as stereotypically feminine.

Warnings and Challenges

Just as directives and criticisms may be delivered in unmitigated, aggravated, or mitigated fashion, so too can warnings and challenges. And as is the case with both directives and criticisms, depending on whether the warning or challenge is unmitigated, aggravated, or mitigated, it can be categorized as being either stereotypically feminine or masculine.

Gina:	I've been getting all of the trade magazines.
Ann:	Yeah, because they are sent to you.
Bill:	But she doesn't pass them on.
Gina:	I do. (laughs)
Bill:	Well, I don't get them.

In this example, Bill negatively evaluates Gina, contesting her authority by issuing an unmitigated criticism ("But she doesn't pass them on.") followed by an unmitigated challenge ("Well, I don't get them.").

Use of Humor

Although humor is not absolutely necessary to get tasks achieved in the workplace, a significant amount of research has been conducted in this area, including the impact of gender on humor.

Humor is multifunctional. It is often used to maintain good working relations in the workplace, though it can also be used strategically to invoke power to produce challenges and subvert existing relations.[34] This type of subversive humor is seen as stereotypically more masculine.

1. Bill:	I didn't realize that we had 20 reams left.	
2. Erin:	uh-huh.	
3. Ann:	[It's not true to say but]	
4. Erin:	[and I can't believe] what you're saying. I told you [about it] (laughs)	
5. Bill:		[oh, right]
	(laughter)	

In line 4, Erin, the participant with the least power and status in the group, engages in stereotypically masculine humor to challenge her superiors by informing them that she can't believe what they are saying since she already told them. She uses laughter to signal humor, which is successfully received with the ensuing laughter.

Humor can also be used to pay attention to face needs by disguising a less acceptable message, such as a directive or criticism. This repressive humor can be seen as more stereotypically feminine.

Gina:	Two o'clock will be the time and that way (smile voice) if you go to the bar then you're not welcome back.
	(laughter)

Gina uses humor in this case to inform the group that they need to leave work for a holiday. The humor as well as a change in her vocal intonation disguises a directive and warns subordinates that they must leave at 2 p.m., since the company will close at that time.

Humor also can be produced jointly. Conjoint humor includes a continuum with a maximally collaborative floor at one end and a minimally collaborative floor at the other. Like individual humor, it can be supportive or unsupportive.

A study of jointly constructed humor found that women do not act simply as a supportive audience to male humor.[35] Women at work participate in the full range of types of conjoint humorous workplace sequences. That is, both women and men used conjoint humor supportively, to elaborate or expand a previous contribution, and unsupportively, to challenge another's humorous assertion.[36] However, the study noted trends that indicated that the presence of women versus men in a meeting had some influence on the overall proportion of the particular kinds of humor exhibited.[37] Supportive conjoint humor, for instance, tended to be more frequent in groups that included women (whether the groups were single or mixed gender).[38] Unsupportive conjoint humor, on the other hand, tended to occur more frequently in meetings in which men were involved (again, whether single or mixed gender).[39] Particularly interesting was the fact that a high energy, maximally shared floor, with frequent turn overlapping and strong cohesive ties between contributions to the conjoint humor, was more likely to develop in contexts where both genders were participants, and least likely in those where only men were present.[40] Conversely, a minimally collaborative, or competitive type of floor tended to develop more often in groups involving only men, or in which men predominated.[41]

Opportunity to Reflect

Think of how humor is used in your workplace. Is humor used differently by women than by men? If so, how? What functions does it perform?

Community of Practice

Thus far, we have discussed the problem of gendered stereotypes in the workplace, their effect particularly on women leaders, and the features of gendered talk. With this knowledge, the real challenge that women (and men) leaders face is attempting to determine how and when to use different types of talk to the best effect. This is largely determined by the community of practice, as was discussed in Chapter 4.

Gender is also produced and reproduced in differential forms of participation in particular communities of practice. Women tend to be subordinate to men in the workplace, for example, women in the military have not traditionally engaged in combat, and in the academy, most theoretical disciplines are overwhelmingly male with women concentrated in descriptive and applied disciplines that "support" theorizing. The relations among communities of practice when they come together in overarching communities of practice also produce gender arrangements.

Holmes[42] has shown that effective female leaders are able to draw expertly on a *repertoire* of linguistic strategies stereotypically coded as masculine and feminine. The critical component, though, in determining their overall effectiveness is how actors are positioned by their community of practice. Like linguistic strategies, a community of practice can be either feminine, that is, supportive and team oriented, or masculine, competitive, and individualistic.

Mullany[43] found numerous examples in her studies of management meetings whereby males use co-operative strategies and females use competitive strategies, dependent on the community of practice in which they were situated. She argues that theorists should take greater account of the norms and conventions of different communities of practice, as well as institutional status, role and corporate discourses, in order to achieve a more finely grained understanding of how different business communities "do leadership." This is not only the task of researchers but also for those who aspire to leadership positions.

Here is an example from our research that indicates how choosing a leadership style that does not match the one preferred by the group may result in a failed attempt at leading. In the example below, S6 who is a female Asian participant in a mixed group, attempts to establish herself as an active participant in the decision-making process using discursive moves characteristic of a Cooperative Leadership Style.

S4:	Alright. See the thing is, I, I think it's more important to survive first before you start moving, cause 50 miles, no matter how fast you walk will still take you like about, um, if you're with all that stuff maybe 5, 6 days. So you have to make sure you can survive first cause no matter what you're gonna have to stop and rest.
	[So] [I figured it would be more important to...]
S3:	[XX]
S6:	[Ya, especially it's, uh...] close to arctic.
S4:	[Ya.]
S3:	[Ya.]

In this example, S6 tries to take the floor by overlapping to acknowledge the contribution of the previous speaker and elaborating on the topic initiated by S4.

S6 does not speak again until a few minutes later in the meeting, when she talks on the topic directly connected to what has been said before: "[I think,] so it's October, close to Arctic, cause I've been to Alaska in the August, uh, the, uh in August the day, there, the day is really long..."

Just as in her first attempt, S6 uses a cooperative overlap and contributes additional content related to the topic under discussion in this example.

| 30. S3: | z Ya that's true. [I was thinking of that] too. |
| 31. S6: | [You have to   ] z take it into consideration. |

In her next turn, S6 receives validation from S3 in line 30 (above), at which point she overlaps again in line 31.

Later on in the discussion, S5 challenges S6 by noting, "September is the fall, um, is the end of September is the equinox. So you're getting about a 12 to 12 at, by October 5th." S6 attempts to defend her statement "October, the day should be much longer than the night," but after S5 continues to pursue her point, S6 finally concedes, "Oh, right." At this point, S3 changes the topic, "Maybe, maybe we should determine what is most useless before what's most important" and S6 overlaps again in agreement, "right." She makes no further attempt to contribute in the meeting.

S6 uses discursive moves that are more characteristic of a Cooperative Leadership Style. She acknowledges the contribution of the previous speaker and connects to and builds upon the previous speaker's topic on all occasions. She uses minimal responses in the form of *yeah* and *mhm* to signal listening.

Unfortunately, this more stereotypically feminine style of leadership as enacted by S6 doesn't gain much traction in this particular group. The more competitive style exhibited by S5 and S3 essentially silences S6.

This example shows that those who aspire to leadership roles need to match their discursive style and moves to those that correspond with the preferences of the group. In other words, just because one has mastered a particular leadership style or can communicate "well," he or she will not necessarily emerge as the leader within a group. Workplace cultures develop their own sets of norms that provide organizational members with a discourse framework within which they must interact.

Regardless of gendered talk preferences, leaders need to develop the skills to analyze and identify the attributes and values of a particular community of practice as well as the type of communication behaviors that are more characteristic of that community and to reproduce them with ease and skill. More broadly, once you reach a position of power, it is imperative that you work to diminish the effect of gender stereotyping—as well as other types—in your workplace.

In fact, Schnurr suggests gender can be brought to the forefront by using humor to make fun of the stereotypes that members sometimes enact or by rejecting and dismissing them.[44] In the following example from Schnurr, Jill uses humor to address stereotypes she has to deal and compete with when interacting in a predominantly masculine environment.

Lucy:	and you're not gonna have a computer monitor
Jill:	I'm not gonna have a monitor
Lucy:	Now you've got room for a pot plant
Jill:	Perfect. There you go
Don:	(laughs)
Jill:	You can tell the girly office, can't you?
Don:	Yes.
Lucy:	(laughs)

In this extract, Jill emphasizes femininity within the boundaries of a predominantly masculine environment, thereby challenging the masculine norm of leadership. Using humor provides an "avenue for a subordinate group to assert their differences while expressing frustration and ambivalence at the effects of marginalization."[45] In effect, Jill challenges the gender stereotypes prevailing in her workplace.

Opportunity to Reflect

In Chapter 3, you were asked to identify your preferred leadership style. As you reflect upon the issues discussed here, would you say that your preferred leadership style is a good match for your community of practice? Why or why not? If not, what specific elements of talk might you change to be a better fit?

Summary

Gender is a social construct, just as is ethnicity or cultural difference, and it is different from biological sex. It is a social patterning that has been created over time and has been passed down from generation to generation within a culture. It is a learned behavior that we enact each day to "create" our gendered selves. Studies have shown that, because of gender stereotypes, women who wish to be seen as leaders face a double bind: if they act like women are supposed to, they are seen as weak. If they take on the attributes associated with men, then they are seen as too aggressive. Neither is a good alternative and hence, the name "double bind": a situation in which a person—in this case, a woman—must choose between equally unsatisfactory alternatives.

Dozens of studies have identified elements of gendered communication. Stereotypically feminine interactional styles tend to be facilitative, supportive, conciliatory, indirect, collaborative, publicly modest, and affectively oriented. Stereotypically masculine interactional styles, on the other hand, tend to be competitive, aggressively interrupting, confrontational, direct, autonomous, publicly dominating, and task oriented. While women's voices combine and overlap, male friends prefer a one-at-a-time pattern of talking, with one speaker holding the floor at any given time. Men also hedge less and use questions to seek information from each other.

Women's talk tends to involve discussion of highly personal issues, while men tend to prefer less impersonal topics that allow participants to take turns at being the expert. Women in positions of authority will be more likely to issue directives in a face-saving manner, by using such tactics as indirectness to avoid potentially confrontational reactions. Other speech acts that can be seen as stereotypically feminine are mitigating directives, criticisms, warnings, and challenges.

The real challenge that both women and men leaders face is determining how and when to use different types of talk to the best effect. Effective female leaders are able to draw expertly on a repertoire of linguistic strategies stereotypically coded as masculine and feminine. The critical component, though, in determining their overall effectiveness is how actors are positioned by their community of practice. As with linguistic strategies, a community of practice can be either feminine, that is, supportive and team oriented, or masculine, competitive and individualistic. For instance, males may use co-operative strategies and females may use competitive strategies, dependent on the community of practice in which they were situated. Those who aspire to leadership should take greater account of the norms and conventions of different communities of practice, as well as institutional status, role and corporate discourses, in order to achieve a more finely grained understanding of how different business communities "do leadership."

CHAPTER 7

Applying the Discursive Approach and Beyond

The most dangerous leadership myth is that leaders are born—that there is a genetic factor to leadership. That's nonsense; in fact, the opposite is true. Leaders are made rather than born.

—Warren Bennis

In this book, we have illustrated some key elements of discourse and how they may contribute to or detract from the emergence of leadership. Understanding and being able to identify these elements is one thing—being able to put them into practice is another. We introduced the idea of communities of practice, which underscored the importance of analyzing and understanding the context of communication in order to interact effectively and considered the effects of culture in terms of cross-cultural leadership, and gender.

In this final chapter, we will discuss the abilities you need to use effectively what you have learned about discourse. These abilities include strategic orientation, cultural and self-awareness, and critical mindedness. We will also introduce additional nonverbal communication issues that deserve attention for successful leadership enactment.

Strategic Communication

As we have suggested, it is important for you to be aware of the context of the communication as well as the actors involved in order to determine the most successful talk practices. Barbara J. O'Keefe has identified three communicator styles that relate to how we produce messages, assess the communication cues of others, and adapt our messages accordingly. These styles are referred to as Expressive, Conventional, and Rhetorical or Strategic.[1]

An Expressive will likely find it challenging to understand the importance of the context of communication in producing messages. That is because the Expressive's goal is authentic expression free of expectations of polite discussion. Expressives often are blunt, surprising, or even embarrassing. On the plus side, Expressives are often viewed as believable and trustworthy because of their lack of guile. They are more concerned with expressing their true feelings than adapting to the situation.

Conventionals have some sensitivity to the issue of the context of communication because they do what is appropriate to the situation and follow social norms. The weakness of Conventionals is that it can sometimes be difficult for them to see the nuanced differences of situations. Conventionals tend to see others as being like themselves, so they tend to minimize or overlook the differences in situations and consequently minimize the opportunity to shape meaning or construct reality.

The Strategic has a heightened sensitivity to the power of language and thus intentionally selects words and actions to make a particular impact. Unlike a Conventional, the Strategic can see alternative ways of interpreting situations and is confident in acting to shape or control them. The Strategic is also referred to as Rhetorical since this approach provides a systematic way of analyzing communicative situations. Using the rhetorical approach involves analyzing the context and the audience, identifying the purposes for communicating, and thus adapting the message to suit the situation.

In terms of leadership, O'Keefe's argues that Expressives appear to be the least adaptable in terms of their ability to use other styles, while Conventionals can also apply the Expressive style. Strategics can exhibit all three styles, given their ability to use language and other communication practices to their advantage.

Opportunity to Reflect

Go to http://www.iabc.com/education/pdf/CommunicationsStyleIn ventory.pdf and download the Communication Styles Inventory to determine your preferred style. Then consider the following: Were you surprised by the outcome of the inventory? If you are not a Strategic, what might you do to become more aware of differing perspectives and shape your communication to better account for these differences?

Cultural Intelligence

Globalization has had a dramatic effect on the business environment in which we now operate. Globalization has impacted the diversity of the workforce as well as increased interdependency of national, international, and multinational corporations and their employees. These changes underscore the importance of the ability to understand the diversity in others and communicate with them effectively.

One construct that aids in understanding the formation of global communication skills is the notion of *cultural intelligence*. Even though you may never work in a foreign country, you will interact with others whose backgrounds, experience, and values differ, perhaps widely, from your own. Understanding cultural intelligence is thus helpful in developing a mindset conducive to operating in a diverse business world and emerging as a global leader. Cultural intelligence includes the following elements:

- **Cognitive knowledge**: The possession of a wide-ranging information base about a variety of people and their cultural customs.
- **Motivation**: Healthy self-efficacy, persistence, goals, value questioning, and integration.
- **Behavioral adaptability**: The capacity to interact in a wide range of situations, environments, and diverse groups.[2]

Becoming culturally intelligent involves learning about other people and developing a respect for their differing beliefs and values. It involves developing global business savvy and a cosmopolitan outlook. It requires being motivated to learn about others and able to adapt to different environments and groups of people. Other specific traits and competencies associated with cultural intelligence are self-monitoring (discussed in the next section), holding non-ethnocentric attitudes, and being open to experience. These same skills are needed to be able to apply effectively the discursive approach discussed in this book. Understanding others and the context of communication and adapting your own interactional practices to suit the situation are necessary not only for effective communication but for successful leadership enactment, regardless of the theoretical or conceptual approach you apply.

The Global Literacy Competence (GLC) model (Figure 7.1) offers a road map to begin to conceptualize the stages of cultural intelligence development.[3]

The preceding model illustrates that understanding others and learning to adapt to different situations is a process that requires an attitude of openness and dedication to learning and change. A high level of self-awareness and "other" awareness is needed, along with the ability to observe others and our surroundings and analyze what is occurring in the moment of interaction.

This ability to develop "other" awareness can be challenging for those who have reached adulthood in an individualist culture such as the United States. As we discussed in Chapter 5, in such a culture, the focus is on the needs of the individual rather than the group or groups to which we belong. This focus on the self can make it challenging to understand and appreciate other perspectives. In addition, the United States tends to be a low-context culture, which means that we generally pay little attention to the context of communication. Therefore, to be effective at applying the knowledge you have gained about discursive leadership practices, it is likely that you will need to develop a greater sensitivity to your environment, which will likely occur in multiple steps, as the GLC model illustrates.

Self and Other Awareness

To be an effective communicator, we must develop high levels of *self-awareness*, including our attitudes, values, beliefs, strengths, and weaknesses. If we are to communicate well, it is important to understand how our actions and communication behaviors affect others and how others respond to us and perceive us. It is also important to understand our own values so that we can contrast and compare them with those of others, which can lead to greater clarity regarding differences and similarities.

Self-awareness is developed in two ways: by communicating with one's self and by communicating with others. Communication with ourselves is called *intrapersonal communication*, which includes "our perceptions, memories, experiences, feelings, interpretations, inferences, evaluations, attitudes, opinions, ideas, strategies, images, and states of consciousness."[4]

Figure 7.1 Levels of global communication competence

Level	Description
1. Awareness	In this novice stage, exposure leads to vague impressions of which people are barely conscious. At this level, there is little or no sense-making but a dawning awareness of something different and possibly interesting, strange, frightening, or annoying.
2. Understanding	Individuals begin to exhibit some conscious effort to learn why people are the way they are and why people do what they do. They display interest in those who are different from themselves. Sanchez et. al. (2000) refers to this as the "transition stage." In this stage, the individual collects information through reading, observation, and real experiences, as well as by asking questions to learn more about the new cultural phenomenon.
3. Appreciation	Individuals begin to take a "leap of faith" and experience a genuine tolerance of different points of view. Through understanding basic differences as well as areas where one thinks, acts, and reacts similarly, a positive feeling towards the "new" cultural phenomenon begins to form. Individuals not only put up with the "new" culture, but also display a genuine appreciation of and, in some cases, preference for certain aspects of the "new" culture.
4. Acceptance	The possibility of interaction between cultures increases appreciably. People are more sophisticated both in terms of recognizing commonalities and in terms of effectively dealing with differences. At this stage, there is willingness to acquire new patterns of behavior and attitudes. This is a departure from the ethnocentric notion that "my way is the best way and the only way."
5. Internalization	The individual goes beyond making sense of information and actually embarks on a deliberate internalization process with profound positive feelings for the once unknown cultural phenomenon. At this stage, there is a clear sense of self-understanding leading to readiness to act and interact with the locals/nationals in a natural, appropriate, and culturally effective manner.
6. Adaptation	Cultural competence becomes a way of life. It is internalized to the degree that it is out of one's consciousness, and thus becomes effortless and second nature. Individuals at this level display and possess the 1) capacity for gathering knowledge about different cultures, 2) drive or motivation to adapt, and 3) behavioral adaptability—the capacity to act effectively based upon their knowledge and motivation.

Source: Chin, Gu and Tubbs (2001). pp 20–35.

Intrapersonal intelligence is the capacity to form an accurate model of one's self and to be able to use that model to operate effectively in life. Intrapersonal intelligence is developed by reflecting on our thoughts and actions to understand what motivates those thoughts and actions.[5]

Another way to think about the ability to use an accurate self model to operate effectively in life or more strategically is that it involves the ability to manage the impressions we make upon others. This ability to "shape reality" at a personal level is known as *impression management*. According to this theory, any individual or organization must establish and maintain impressions that are congruent with the perceptions they want to convey to their publics.[6] Impression management encompasses the vital ways in which we establish and communicate this congruence between personal or organizational goals and our intended actions. This process creates public perception.

People concerned with their expressive self-presentation tend to closely monitor themselves in order to ensure appropriate or desired public appearances. Such individuals are categorized as *high self-monitors* and often behave in a manner that is highly responsive to social cues and their situational context.[7] High self-monitors can be thought of as social pragmatists who project images in an attempt to impress others and receive positive feedback.[8] In leadership research, self-monitoring is seen as an indicator of flexibility and responsiveness to social situations. It has been shown that high self-monitors get promoted most often, but that women score lower on self-monitoring than men. High self-monitors might be viewed as what O'Keefe describes as Strategics.

Conversely, low self-monitors do not participate, to the same degree, in expressive control and are not highly concerned about situational appropriateness.[9] Low self-monitors tend to exhibit expressive controls congruent with their own internal states, that is, beliefs, attitudes, and dispositions, regardless of social circumstance. Low self-monitors are often less observant of social context and consider expressing a self-presentation dissimilar from their internal states as a falsehood and undesirable.[10] Low self-monitors might correspond to what O'Keefe calls Expressives.

The correlate of intrapersonal intelligence, ***interpersonal intelligence***,[11] is the ability to understand other people: what motivates them, how they work, and how to work cooperatively with them. People with strong interpersonal intelligence are skilled at assessing emotions, motivations, desires, and intentions of those around them. They are not only good at communicating verbally, but they also pay attention to the nonverbal communication cues and messages of others. They are able to see situations from different perspectives and create positive relationships with others as well as resolve conflicts. Interpersonal intelligence is also a requirement for strategic communication.

Observational and Listening Skills

Effective analysis of the context of communication as well as those involved requires excellent observation skills. Developing good observation skills involves watching and listening to others intently and registering what you see or hear.

In addition to developing self-awareness and knowledge of others, behaviors and habits essential to accurate observation include the following:

- Sizing up people by "people watching"
- Developing clarity or the ability to see the world as it is
- Fostering curiosity by asking why
- Practicing good listening
- Setting aside personal biases
- Seeking the inputs of others
- Seeking out new experiences and possibilities
- Being comfortable with ambiguity[12]

One way to enhance your ability to observe and focus is to take field notes of what you see. Try this in your next meeting: describe what is happening, including participants' appearances and their verbal and nonverbal communication cues. Take a moment after the meeting to analyze your notes to identify any overarching themes that may not have been brought into the open during the discussion. Being able to identify these broader issues is the mark of strategic thinking and diverges from a focus on the details.

Part of developing good observational skills is to develop good listening habits. Not only are good listening skills needed for understanding the context and those involved, listening is the communication activity that businesspeople spend the most time doing. In general, businesspeople spend nearly 33% of their time listening, about 26% of their time speaking, and nearly 19% of their time reading.[13] Executives may spend more time listening—as much as 80% of their day.[14] Although we spend a majority of our communication time listening the skill often receives little attention. In a survey conducted by a corporate training and development firm, 80% of the corporate executives who responded rated listening as the most important skill in the workforce. However, nearly 30% said that listening was the communication skill most lacking in their employees.[15]

Listening does not mean the same thing as hearing. Hearing is the sensory ability to receive sound and generally requires no effort or energy on our part. We receive and hear sounds constantly. However, listening is a more active, engaged process. According to the International Listening Association, listening is "the active process of receiving, constructing meaning from, and responding to spoken and/or nonverbal messages. It involves the ability to retain information, as well as to react empathically and/or appreciatively to spoken and/or nonverbal messages." Listening requires energy and effort, whereas hearing is automatic and passive.

We tend to be poor listeners for a number of reasons. We may be distracted by the external environment or by internal factors. We may be ill or tired, or we may have other tasks that need our attention. A speaker may say something that triggers a negative emotion in us and we may tune out or turn our attention to formulating our rebuttal. Another big problem is that we think much faster than a person can speak. Because of these distractions or barriers, listeners need training to slow down the mental processes and focus on what others are saying.

One way to become a better listener is to practice active listening. Active listening is "listening with a purpose."[16] It involves the following four steps:

1. Listen carefully by using all available senses, including observation.
2. Paraphrase what is heard both mentally and verbally so you can clarify and remember the information. Paraphrasing involves such statements as "If I hear you correctly, you are saying. . . ."

3. Check your understanding to ensure accuracy. To check understanding, you might follow your paraphrased statement by asking, "Is that right?"
4. Provide feedback to the speaker, both verbally and nonverbally.

Feedback can be either positive or negative. Positive feedback consists of the listener's verbal and nonverbal responses that are intended to affirm the speaker and his or her message, while negative feedback consists of a listener's verbal and nonverbal responses that are intended to disaffirm the speaker and the message. In productive communication situations, negative feedback generally should not be used to disaffirm the speaker or discredit the message, because this may negatively affect your relationship and your ability to communicate effectively in the future.

Analytical Thinking Skills

Developing the facility to move from a focus on details to the ability to identify broader overarching issues is an analytical skill, one that is critically needed in an age in which most of us are overwhelmed by the sheer amount of information presented to us each day. In fact, more information is generated worldwide in a twenty-four-hour period than you could process and absorb in all your years on Earth. With the expansion of the Internet, we are approaching a point in which more information will be generated in one hour than could be processed and absorbed in your lifetime.[17]

The corresponding overload affects our ability to gather, analyze, and identify information needed for sound decisions and effective communication. In other words, the sheer volume of available information makes it easy to get "lost in the trees." Good communicator must also be able to distance themselves from the data and consider how the information might be synthesized into a broader, more coherent meaning. Higher-order thinking skills needed for strategic thinking go beyond merely absorbing information. They involve the ability to comprehend, apply, analyze, synthesize, and evaluate information, the latter three abilities being part of the critical thinking that is necessary for strategic thinking[18] (see Figure 7.2).

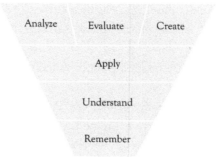

Figure 7.2. A taxonomy of cognitive skills from highest to lowest.

Source: Krathwohl (2002). pp. 212–218.

Opportunity to Reflect

Go to http://www.queendom.com/queendom_tests/transfer and take the Analytical Reasoning Test. Then consider the following: Were you surprised by the outcome of the test? What methods might you use to enhance your analytical reasoning skills?

Nonverbal Communication

One facet of communication we have not yet directly addressed is non-verbal communication or what we commonly call "body language" (although this term does not encompass all of the aspects of nonverbal communication). Because a discursive approach to leadership focuses on talk, this element of communication has not been a critical focus in this book. However, we would be remiss not to discuss the importance of nonverbal cues in our ability to enact leadership.

Developing an awareness of nonverbal communication is impor-tant, because during face-to-face communication, most of the infor-mation that is provided comes in the form of nonverbal cues. In fact, some say that nonverbal cues provide 93% of the meaning exchanged in face-to-face communication situations such as oral presentations and meetings. Of that percentage, 35% of the meaning comes from tone of voice, whereas 58% comes from gestures, facial expressions, and other physical cues.

These statistics mean that to be believable and credible, business communicators must *act* the way they want to be perceived by others. This notion is reflected in the adage "actions speak louder than words." It is, therefore, important to ensure ***strategic alignment*** between your oral messages and your nonverbal ones.

In nonverbal communication, the communication signals are multiple and simultaneous. These signals include information that we receive from another person's voice, facial expressions and eyes, body posture, movement, appearance, use of space, use of time, touching, clothing, and other artifacts.

Paralanguage

Paralanguage refers to the rate, pitch, and volume qualities of the voice that interrupt or temporarily take the place of speech and affect the meaning of a message.[19] Paralanguage includes such vocal qualifiers as pitch (high or low); intensity (loud or soft); extent (drawls and accents); emotional characterizers, such as laughing or crying; and segregates, such as saying "uh," "um," or "uh-huh." Some vocal qualifiers may communicate emotion; for example, in the United States, increased volume or rate may indicate anger.

Cultural differences exist in the use and meanings of paralanguage. For instance, Arabs speak loudly to indicate strength and sincerity, while Filipinos speak softly to indicate good breeding and education. Italians and Arabs speak more rapidly than Americans, and Americans are louder than Europeans.

The lack of vocalization, or silence, also communicates differing meanings depending on culture. People in the United States, Germany, France, and Southern Europe are uncomfortable with silence. People in East Asia consider silence an important part of business and social discourse and not a failure to communicate. Silence in Finland and East Asia is associated with listening and learning; silence protects privacy and individualism and shows respect for the privacy and individualism of others.[20]

Bodily Movement and Facial Expression

The study of posture, movement, gestures, and facial expression is called **kinesics**. As with many aspects of communication, the meaning of body movements and facial expressions differ by culture. Although many people, particularly men, in the United States may sprawl when they are seated and slouch when they stand, such postures would be considered rude in Germany. Crossing the legs or feet is common in the United States, but doing so in the Middle East is inappropriate, because showing the sole of your shoe or bottom of your foot to someone is considered rude.

Gestures have different meanings depending on the culture, too. In the United States, people generally gesture moderately, whereas Italians, Greeks, and some Latin Americans use more dramatic gestures when speaking. The Chinese and Japanese, in contrast, tend to keep their hands and arms close to their bodies when speaking. The use of facial expressions are also culturally distinct. In China, people rarely express emotion, whereas the Japanese may smile to show a variety of emotions, such as happiness, sadness, or even anger.

Gaze and eye contact also differ by culture. People from the United States, Canada, Great Britain, and Eastern Europe favor direct eye contact. In these cultures, eye contact is considered a sign of respect and attentiveness. People who avoid contact may be considered, untrustworthy, unfriendly, inattentive, insecure, or inattentive.[21] People from Germany and the Middle East favor direct eye contact, but the gaze is so intense it may make people otherwise accustomed to direct eye contact uncomfortable. In some other countries, respect is shown by avoiding direct eye contact. These countries include Japan, China, Indonesia, Latin America, the Caribbean, and parts of Africa. In Egypt, there is no eye contact between men and women who do not know each other, and in India, eye contact is avoided between people of different socioeconomic levels.[22]

Albert Mehrabian studied nonverbal communication in the United States by examining the concepts of liking, status, and responsiveness of people in communication situations. He found the following:

- **Liking** was often expressed by leaning forward, standing face to face and in close proximity, increased touching, relaxed posture, open arms and body, positive facial expression, and eye contact.

- **High status** or power is communicated nonverbally by less eye contact and taking up more space through bigger gestures and a relaxed posture, including when sitting. This is an important issue for women and people from other cultures to consider, since they may have been socialized to appear small by taking up less space.
- **Responsiveness** is exhibited nonverbally by moving toward the other person, using spontaneous gestures, shifting posture and position, and facial expressiveness. The face and body should provide positive feedback to those with whom you are communicating.

Thus, body language is a strong indicator of the extent to which communicators like one another are interested in each other's views. In addition, it indicates the perceived status, or power relationship, between the communicators.

Differences in body language have also been found between men and women. In U.S. studies, men tend to exhibit an informal demeanor when speaking to women, relaxed posture, and close personal space. They are likely to, touch, stare, and ignore, as well as avoid smiling.[23] Women are circumspect in demeanor when speaking to men, have tense body posture, use distant personal space, avoid touching others, avert their eyes, watch others, smile, and show emotional expression.[24]

Awareness of the significance and potential impact of nonverbal communication behaviors can increase your ability to establish credibility and build a positive relationship with your audience in face-to-face communication situations.

Bodily Appearance

Our body type and physical attractiveness also affect our ability to communicate with others. Body type, or **somatotype**, is comprised of a combination of height, weight, and muscularity. Tall people are generally more successful and are viewed more positively by others. Taller people are more likely to be hired in employment interviews, and they tend to have higher incomes.[25] Regarding attractiveness, women generally find tall men more attractive than short ones; however, they view men of medium height as the most attractive and likeable. Those who are short, soft, and round are often judged negatively in terms of their personalities and their concern about self-presentation.

Particular physical characteristics are considered as universal aspects of attractiveness: bright eyes, symmetrical facial features, and a thin or medium build.[26] Physical attractiveness generally leads to more social success in adulthood; attractive people receive higher initial credibility ratings than do those who are viewed as unattractive.[27] Physically attractive people are more likely to be hired and to receive higher salaries.[28] However, these views may not be consistent for gender. Studies have shown that attractive females are sometimes judged as less competent than less attractive females.[29]

Even though there is little that we can do to change our height, we can control to some degree our body type and our attractiveness by applying good grooming and conveying a positive attitude.

Use of Space

The study of human space, or **proxemics**, revolves around two concepts: territoriality and personal space. **Territoriality** refers to your need to establish and maintain certain spaces as your own. In a workplace environment, the walls of your cubicle or office often establish your territory. **Personal space** is the distance between you and others with which you feel comfortable. When someone invades your personal space, you often automatically move away from that person. Personal space preferences do differ among individuals; for example, large people usually prefer more space, as do men. Similarly, personal space preferences differ by culture. People of the United States tend to need more space than those from Greece, Latin America, or the Middle East. The Japanese tend to prefer a greater distance in social situations than do people of the United States.

Anthropologist Edward T. Hall defined four distances people use when they communicate. **Intimate distance** in the United States is used more in private than in public and extends to about 18 inches. This distance is used to communicate affection, give comfort, and to protect. A **personal distance** range of 18 inches to 4 feet is typically used by those in the United States for conversation and non intimate exchanges. **Social distance for Americans** ranges from 4 feet to 8 feet and is used for professional communication. The higher the status of the person, generally the greater the social distance he or she maintains. **Public distance** exceeds 12 feet and is used most often for public speaking.

Your relationship to other people is related to your use of space. You stand closer to friends and farther from enemies, strangers, authority figures, high-status people, physically challenged people, and people from different racial groups than your own. The effectiveness of communication, or the way you respond to others, can be affected by personal space violations. What this knowledge means for those who are leaders or who aspire to be leaders is that we must be attentive to our use of space. As mentioned earlier, this is particularly true for a woman since studies have shown that women tend to take up less space than men, which may sabotage their efforts to be seen as powerful. Even though many women may be of smaller stature than some men, they can better claim their space by squaring their shoulders, pulling themselves up to their full height, using larger gestures, and when in presentation situations, using the entire room. They can also work to create an authoritative voice that commands respect. These techniques may also apply to those from cultures that tend to take up less bodily space.

Cultural differences also extend to how people communicate through space in seating arrangements and the layout of offices. People in the United States, for example, prefer to converse face to face, while people in China prefer to sit side by side. This preference may allow them to avoid direct eye contact, which is the custom in that culture. In terms of the office environment, private offices have more status in the United States, while in Japan, only executives of the highest rank may have a private office, although it is just as likely that they have desks in large work areas.[30] In the United States and Germany, the top floor of office buildings is generally occupied by top-level executives, while in France, high-ranking executives occupy the middle of an office area with subordinates located around them.[31]

Time

Chronemics, or values related to time, refers to the way that people organize and use time and the messages that are created because of our organization and use of time. Our use of time communicates several messages. Our urgency or casualness with the starting time of an event could be an indication of our personality, our status, or our culture. Highly structured, task-oriented people may arrive and leave on time, whereas relaxed, relation-oriented people may arrive and leave late. People with low status are expected to be on time, whereas those with higher status are granted more leeway in their arrival time. Being on time is more important in some cultures than others; for example, being on time is more important in North America than in South America, whereas people of Germany and Switzerland are even more time-conscious than people from the United States.

Another cultural issue to recognize is whether a country follows **polychromic time (P-time)** or **monochromic time** (M-time). Cultures that follow polychromic time are comfortable working on several activities simultaneously. People are viewed as more important than schedules, so the interruptions are acceptable. People in polychromic cultures borrow and lend things and tend to build lifelong relationships. People from high-context cultures tend to be polychromic, including those from Latin America, the Middle East, and Southern Europe.[32]

In monochromic cultures, time is considered as something tangible as is reflected in such sayings as "wasting time" and "time is money." Time is seen as linear and manageable in such cultures. It is considered rude to do two things at once, such as answering the phone while someone is in your office or stopping to text someone while in a conversation, though this expectation is rapidly changing. Monochromic people tend to respect private property and rarely borrow or lend and are accustomed to short-term relationships.[33] Countries that are monochromic in their time orientation include the United States, Germany, Switzerland, and England.

Touching

Haptics, or touch, communicates a great deal. Norms for touching and the tendency to touch differs by gender and culture. Studies indicate that women in the United States value touch more than men, women are touched more than men, men touch others more than women do, and men may use touch to indicate power or dominance.[34]

People of various cultures handle touch differently. Sidney Jourard determined the rates of touch per hour among adults of various cultures and found that adults in Puerto Rico touched 180 times per hour; those in Paris touched about 110 times an hour; those in Gainesville, Florida, touched 2 times per hour; and those in London touched once per hour.[35] In touch-oriented cultures, such as those of Italy, Spain, Portugal, and Greece, both males and females may walk arm in arm or hold hands. In Mexico, Eastern Europe, and the Arab world, embracing and kissing is common. However, in Hong Kong, initiating any public physical contact should be avoided.[36]

Some cultures also restrict where touching may occur on the body. In India and Thailand, it is offensive to touch the head because it is considered sacred. In Korea, young people do not touch the shoulders of elders.[37]

Clothing and Other Artifacts

Your clothing and other adornments, such as jewelry, hairstyle, cosmetics, shoes, glasses, tattoos, and body piercings communicate to others a perception of your age, gender, status, role, socioeconomic class, group memberships, personality, and relation to the opposite sex. Such cues can also indicate the historical period, the time of day, and the climate. Conforming to current styles has been correlated to a person's desire to be accepted and liked by others.[38] On a deeper level, clothing and other artifacts communicate your self-concept or the type of person you believe you are.[39]

Clothing is important in forming first impressions[40] and has been shown to affect others' impressions of our status and personality traits.[41] For this reason, general advice is to pay attention to dressing professionally in business situations because it can affect your credibility, attractiveness, and perceived ability to fit within a professional culture. This guideline can be particularly important when dealing with audiences from other cultures because they tend to make assumptions about another person's education level, status, and income based upon dress alone.[42]

This section has provided a brief summary of the nonverbal elements of communication and how they might be interpreted by differing cultures. Although not the focus of this book, it is important to recognize the potential impact of nonverbal communication cues on how others perceive us. As a strategic communicator, one who marshals language to shape organizational realities, attention must be paid also to the potentially symbolic nature of all aspects of our environment.

Opportunity to Reflect

Create a short presentation that you can video-record using your smartphone or video camera. Record the presentation and then review it to analyze your nonverbal cues. Do you look confident and composed? Professional, yet approachable? If not, what are the nonverbal cues that you need to change to make the most favorable impression? Try practicing these nonverbal elements in your daily interactions.

Summary

In this final chapter, we discussed the abilities you need to use what you have learned about discourse effectively. It is important to be aware of the context of the communication as well as the actors involved in determining how to proceed in terms of producing the most successful talk practices.

Barbara J. O'Keefe identified three communicator styles that help to illustrate how we produce messages, assess the communication cues of others, and adapt our messages accordingly. Expressives will likely find it challenging to understand the importance of the context of communication in producing messages because their goal is authentic expression free of some of the conventions of polite discussion. Conventionals have some sensitivity to the issue of the context of communication because they do what is appropriate to the situation and follow social norms. The Strategic has a heightened sensitivity to the power of language and thus intentionally selects words and actions to make a particular impact.

In order to be more strategic, one must develop high levels of self-awareness or an understanding of the self, including one's attitudes, values, beliefs, strengths, and weaknesses. Self-awareness is developed in two ways: by communicating with one's self (intrapersonal communication) and by communicating with others (interpersonal communication). Having a high self-awareness enables us to better manage the impressions we make upon others. This ability to "shape reality" at a personal level is known as impression management.

People concerned with their expressive self-presentation tend to closely monitor themselves in order to ensure appropriate or desired public appearances. These high self-monitors often behave in a manner that is highly responsive to social cues and their situational context. In contrast, low self-monitors tend to exhibit expressive controls congruent with their own internal states, that is, beliefs, attitudes, and dispositions regardless of social circumstance.

Effective analysis of the context of communication as well as those involved requires excellent observation skills. Developing good observation skills involves watching and listening to others intently and registering what you see or hear. Also needed are higher order thinking skills that include the ability to comprehend, apply, analyze, synthesize, and evaluate information.

While nonverbal communication is not a consistent area of study in the discursive approach, it is essential to the process. During face-to-face communication, much of the information that is provided comes in the form of nonverbal cues, that are multiple and simultaneous. These signals include information that we receive from another person's voice, facial expressions and eyes; body posture, movement, and appearance; the use of space; the use of time; touching; and clothing, and other artifacts.

Learning to see talk and other communication behaviors as constructing much of our social world, including how people perceive and respond to us, can be extraordinarily useful in constructing a leadership persona in the workplace. Developing the ability to focus on interactions and analyze how they shape reality from moment to moment can provide you the opportunity to more proactively guide that shaping to better reach your professional goals as well as those of the organization.

Notes

Preface

1. Macionis and Gerber (2010).
2. Larrain (1979), p. 197.
3. Burr (1995).

Chapter 1

1. Robbins (2001).
2. Geier (1967).
3. Yukl and Van Fleet (1992), p. 150.
4. Burns (1978).
5. House (1976).
6. Fairhurst and Grant (2010).
7. Carroll and Gillen (1987).
8. Fairhurst (2007).
9. Sigman (1992).
10. Shotter (1993).
11. Clifton (2012a).
12. Knights and Wilmott (1992).
13. Biggart and Hamilton (1987).
14. Robinson (2001).
15. Fairhurst (2007).

Chapter 2

1. Jian, Schmisseur, and Fairhurst (2008), p. 304.
2. Bakeman and Gottman (1986).
3. Aritz and Walker (2009); Aritz and Walker (2010).
4. Johnstone (2002).
5. Tannen (1990).
6. Tannen (1990).
7. Heritage (1984).
8. Tannen (1990).
9. Coates (1993).
10. Sacks (1984), p. 24.

11. Sacks (1986).
12. Clifton (2012b).
13. Clifton (2012b).
14. Schegloff and Sacks (1973).
15. Clifton (2012b).
16. Antaki, Condor, and Levine (1996), p. 488.
17. Fairhurst (2007).
18. French and Raven (1959).

Chapter 3

1. Walker and Aritz (2014).
2. Sacks, Schegloff, and Jefferson (1974).
3. Svennevig (2008), p. 535.
4. Coates (1993).
5. Tannen (1990); Coates (1993).
6. Carson, Tesluk, and Marrone (2007).
7. Vine, Holmes, Marra, Pfeifer, and Jackson (2008).
8. Berger and Luckmann (1967).

Chapter 4

1. Aaltio and Mills (2002); Jenkins (1996), p. 134.
2. Schnurr (2009).
3. Eckert and McConnell-Ginet (1992).
4. Eckert and McConnell-Ginet (1992).
5. Wenger (1998), p. 245.
6. Modaff and DeWine (2002), p. 88.
7. Frost, Moore, Louis, Lundberg, and Martin (1991).
8. Hickman (1998); Schein (1992).
9. Neuhauser, Bender, and Stromberg (2000); Parry and Proctor-Thomson (2003); Schein (1992).
10. Chatman and Jehn (1994); O'Reilly, Chatman, and Caldwell (1993).
11. Schnurr (2009).
12. Schnurr (2009), p. 92.
13. Hay (1995); Seckman and Couch (1989).
14. Schnurr (2009).
15. Clifton (2012a).
16. Sacks, Schegloff, and Jefferson (1974).
17. Clifton (2012a), p. 152.

18. Clifton (2012a), p. 152.
19. Clifton (2012a), p. 152.
20. Clifton (2012a), p. 158.
21. Clifton (2012a), p. 161.
22. Goffman (1959).
23. Clifton (2012b).
24. Schegloff (1980).
25. Clifton (2012b), p. 292.
26. Heritage (1984a), p. 272.
27. Clifton (2012b), p. 301.
28. Austin (1990); Hay (1995).
29. Kotthoff (1996).
30. Holmes and Marra (2002).
31. Holmes and Marra (2006).
32. Holmes and Marra (2006).
33. Holmes and Marra (2006).
34. Holmes and Marra (2006).
35. Holmes and Marra (2006), p. 126.
36. Holmes and Marra (2006), p. 126.
37. Holmes and Marra (2006), p. 127.
38. Collinson (1988); Seckman and Couch (1989); Yarwood (1995).
39. Holmes and Marra (2006).
40. Holmes and Marra (2006).
41. Brown and Levinson (1987).
42. Brown and Levinson (1987), p. 128.
43. Holmes and Marra (2006).
44. Kotthoff (1999).
45. Holmes and Marra (2006), p. 129.
46. Holmes and Marra (2006).
47. Holmes and Marra (2006), p. 130.
48. Rahim and Bonoma (1979).
49. Jacobs (2002); Clayman (2002); Heritage (2002).
50. Kangasharju (2002); Kaufmann (2002); Kakavá (2002).
51. Holmes and Marra (2004).
52. Holmes and Marra (2004), p. 448.

Chapter 5

1. Gudykunst and Ting-Toomey (1988).
2. Hofstede (1980).
3. Hui and Triandis (1986).

4. Hofstede (1980).
5. Triandis (1990).
6. Javidan, Dorfman, de Luque, and House (2006); Brodbeck et al. (2000).
7. House, Hanges, Javidan, Dorfman, and Gupta (2004).
8. Farh and Cheng (2000), p. 94.
9. Farh and Cheng (2000), p. 94.
10. Gelfand, Erez, and Aycan (2007).
11. Pellegrini and Scandura (2008, June).
12. Hui and Tan (1996).
13. Sarros and Santora (2001).
14. Pellegrini and Scandura (2008).
15. Pellegrini, Scandura, and Jayaraman (2010).
16. Forsyth (2009).
17. Bass and Avolio (1994).
18. Shahin and Wright (2004).
19. Casimir, Waldman, Bartram, and Yang (2006).
20. Du-Babcock (1999).
21. Clyne (1994).
22. Yamada (1992).
23. Aritz and Walker (2010).
24. Tannen (1990).
25. Clyne (1994).
26. Clyne (1994).
27. Charles (2007), p. 274.
28. Charles (2007), p. 274.
29. Clyne (1994).

Chapter 6

1. Wang, Parker, and Taylor (2013).
2. Catalyst (2007).
3. Catalyst (2007).
4. Catalyst (2007).
5. Eagly and Johannesen-Schmidt (2001).
6. Sandberg (2013).
7. Yoder and Kahn (2003); Yoder (2001); Rudman and Glick (2001).
8. Coates (1996, January 22).
9. Coates (1996, January 22).
10. Coates (1996, January 22).
11. Coates (1996, January 22).
12. Coates (1996, January 22).

13. Coates (1996, January 22).
14. Coates (1996, January 22).
15. Edelsky (1993).
16. Edelsky (1993).
17. Coates (2004).
18. Mullany (2007).
19. Edelsky (1993), p. 208.
20. Edelsky (1993), p. 212.
21. Holmes (1995), p. 52.
22. James and Drakich (1993).
23. Stein and Heller (1979); Slater (1966); Capella (1985).
24. Holmes, Stubbe, and Vine (1999).
25. Mullany (2007).
26. Tannen (1994); Holmes (1995); Kendall (2003).
27. Holmes and Stubbes (2003).
28. Holmes (1995).
29. Goodwin (1980).
30. Mullany (2007).
31. Mullany (2007).
32. Mullany (2007).
33. Mullany (2007).
34. Holmes (2000); Holmes and Stubbe (2003).
35. Holmes (2006).
36. Holmes (2006).
37. Holmes (2006).
38. Holmes (2006).
39. Holmes (2006).
40. Holmes (2006).
41. Holmes (2006).
42. Holmes (2006).
43. Mullany (2007).
44. Schnurr (2009).
45. Holmes, Stubbe, and Marra (2003), p. 450.

Chapter 7

1. O'Keefe (1988); O'Keefe (1991); O'Keefe (1992a); O'Keefe (1992b).
2. Earley and Ang (2003).
3. Chin, Gu, and Tubbs (2001).
4. Chin, Gu, and Tubbs (2001).
5. Chin, Gu, and Tubbs (2001).

6. Shedletsky (1989).
7. Gardner and Krechevsky (1993).
8. Goffman (1959).
9. Snyder (1974).
10. Snyder (1974).
11. Snyder (1974).
12. Snyder and Gangestad (2000).
13. Snyder and Gangestad (2000).
14. Cox (n.d.).
15. Weinrauch and Swanda (1975).
16. Nichols and Stevens (1983).
17. Salopek (1999).
18. Barker (1971).
19. Chaney and Martin (2011).
20. Chaney and Martin (2011).
21. Chaney and Martin (2011).
22. Chaney and Martin (2011).
23. Henley (1977); Henley (1995).
24. Henley (1977); Henley (1995).
25. Hensley (1992); Knapp and Hall (1992).
26. Brody (1994, March 21), p. A14.
27. Knapp and Hall (1992); Widgery (1974).
28. Knapp and Hall (1992).
29. Kaplan (1978).
30. Gudykunst and Ting-Toomey (1988).
31. Chaney and Martin (2011).
32. Chaney and Martin (2011).
33. Chaney and Martin (2011).
34. Fisher, Rytting, and Heslin (1976); Jourard and Rubin (1968); Henley (1973–1974).
35. Jourard (1968).
36. Chaney and Martin (2011).
37. Axtell (1998).
38. Taylor and Compton (1968).
39. Fisher (1975).
40. Henricks, Kelley, and Eicher (1968).
41. Douty (1963).
42. Gray (1993).

References

Aaltio, I., & Mills, A. (2002). Organizational culture and gendered identities in content. In I. Aaltio & A. Mills (Eds.), *Gender, identity and the culture of organizations* (pp. 3–18). London: Routledge.

Antaki, C., Condor, S., & Levine, M. (1996). Social identities in talk: Speakers' own orientations. *British Journal of Social Psychology 35*, 473–492.

Aritz, J., & Walker, R. C. (2009). Group composition and communication styles: An analysis of multicultural teams in decision-making meetings. *Journal of Intercultural Communication Research 38*(2), 99–114.

Aritz, J., & Walker, R. C. (2010). Multicultural groups in decision-making meetings: Language proficiency and group performance. *Journal of Asian Pacific Communication 20*(2), 307–321.

Aritz, J., & Walker R. C. (2012). The effects of leadership style on intercultural group communication in decision-making meetings. In P. Heynderickx, S. Dieltjens, G. Jacobs, P. Gillaerts, & E. de Groot (Eds.), *The language factor in international business: New perspectives on research, teaching and practice* (Linguistic Insights series). Bern: Peter Lang.

Austin, P. (1990). Politeness revisited: The dark side. In A. Bell, & J. Holmes (Eds.), *New Zealand Ways of Speaking English* (pp. 276–295). Bristol: Multilingual Matters.

Axtell, R. E. (1998). *Gestures.* New York: John Wiley & Sons, Inc.

Bakeman, R., & Gottman, J. M. (1986). *Observing interaction: An introduction to sequential analysis.* Cambridge: Cambridge University Press.

Barker, L. L. (1971). *Listening behavior.* Englewood Cliffs, NJ: Prentice-Hall.

Bass, B. M., & Avolio, B. J. (1994). *Improving organizational effectiveness through transformational leadership.* Thousand Oaks, CA: Sage.

Berger, P. L., & Luckmann, T. (1967). *The social construction of reality: A treaties on the sociology of knowledge.* New York: Anchor.

Biggart, N. W., & Hamilton, G. G. (1987). An institutional theory of leadership. *Journal of Applied Behavioral Science 23*, 429–442.

Brodbeck, F. C., Frese, M., Akerblom, S., Audia, G., Bakacsi, G., Bendova, H., ..., Wunderer, R. (2000). Cultural variation of leadership prototypes across 22 European countries. *Journal of Occupational and Organizational Psychology 73*, 1–29.

Brody, J. E. (1994, March 21). Notions of beauty transcends culture, new study suggests. *The New York Times*, A14.

Brown, P., & Levinson, S. C. (1987). *Politeness: Some universals in language usage.* Cambridge: Cambridge University Press.

Burns, J. M. (1978). *Leadership.* New York, NY: Harper & Row.

Burr, V. (1995). *An introduction to social constructionism.* London: Routledge.

Capella, J. N. (1985). Controlling the floor in conversation. In A. W. Siegman & S. Feldstein (Eds.), *Multichannel integrations of nonverbal behavior* (pp. 69–103). Hillsdale, NJ: Erlbaum.

Carroll, S. J., & Gillen, D. J. (1987). Are classical management functions useful in describing managerial work? *Academy of Management Review 12,* 38–51.

Carson, J. B., Tesluk, P. E., & Marrone, J. A. (2007). Shared leadership in team: An investigation of antecedent conditions and performance. *Academy of Management Journal 50*(5), 1217–1234.

Catalyst. (2007). *The double-bind dilemma for women in leadership: Damned if you do, doomed if you don't–Catalyst.* Retrieved August 1, 2013, from http://www. catalyst.org/knowledge/double-bind-dilemma-women-leadership-damned-if-you-do-doomed-if-you-dont-0

Chaney, L. H., & Martin, J. S. (2011). *Intercultural business communication* (5th Ed.). Boston: Prentice-Hall.

Chatman, J. A., & Jehn, K. A. (1994). Assessing the relationship between industry characteristics and organizational culture: How different can you be? *Academy of Management Journal 37,* 522–553.

Chin, C. O., Gu, J., & Tubbs, S. (2001). Developing global leadership competencies. *Journal of Leadership Studies 7*(4), 20–35.

Clayman, S. (2002). Disagreements and third parties: Dilemmas of neutralism in panel news interviews. *Journal of Pragmatics 34,* 1385–1402.

Clifton, J. (2012a). A discursive approach to leadership: Doing assessments and managing organizational meanings. *Journal of Business Communication 49*(2), 148–168.

Clifton, J. (2012b). Conversation analysis in dialogue with stocks of interactional knowledge: Facework and appraisal interviews. *Journal of Business Communication 49*(4), 283–311.

Clyne, M. (1994). *Intercultural communication at work: Cultural values in discourse.* Cambridge: Cambridge University Press.

Coates, J. (1993). *Women, men and language* (2nd Ed.). London & New York: Longman.

Coates, J. (1996, January 22). The chattering sexes. *London Times.* Retrieved July 23, 2013, from http://www.timeshighereducation.co.uk/news/the-chattering-sexes/92097.article

Coates, J. (2004). *Women, men and language* (3rd Ed.). Harlow: Pearson.

Collinson, D. (1988). Engineering humour: Masculinity, joking and conflict in shop-floor relations. *Organization Studies 9*(2), 181–199.

Cox, A. (n.d.). *Observation: A critical leadership skill.* Retrieved August 12, 2013, from Ezine Articles: http://ezinearticles.com/?Observation—A-Critical -Leadership-Skill&id=743048

Douty, H. I. (1963). Influence of clothing on perception of persons. *Journal of Home Economics, 55,* 197–202.

Du-Babcock, B. (1999). Topic management and turn taking in professional communication. *Management Communication Quarterly 12,* 544–574.

Eagly, A. H., & Johannesen-Schmidt, M. C. (2001, Winter). The leadership styles of women and men. *Journal of Social Issues 57*(4), 781–797.

Earley. P. C., & Ang, S. (2003) *Cultural intelligence.* Stanford, CA: Stanford University Press.

Eckert, P., & McConnell-Ginet, S. (1992). Think practically and look locally: Language and gender as community-based practice. *Annual Review of Anthropology 21,* 461–490.

Edelsky, C. (1993). Who's got the floor? In D. Tannen (Ed.), *Gender and conversational interaction* (pp. 189–227). New York: Oxford University Press.

Fairhurst, G. T. (2007). *Discursive leadership: In conversation with leadership psychology.* Los Angeles, CA: Sage.

Fairhurst, G. T., & Grant, D. (2010). The social construction of leadership: A sailing guide. *Management Communication Quarterly 24*(2), 171–210.

Farh, J. L., & Cheng, B. S. (2000). A cultural analysis of paternalistic leadership in Chinese organization. In J. Li, A. Tsui, & E. Weldon (Eds.), *Management and organizations in the chinese Context* (pp. 84–130). New York, NY: St. Martin's Press, Inc.

Fisher, J. D., Rytting, M., & Heslin, R. (1976). Hands touching hands: Affective and evaluative effects of interpersonal touch. *Sociometry 3,* 416–421.

Fisher, P. (1975). The future's past. *New Literary History 6,* 587–606.

Forsyth, D. R. (2009). *Group dynamics.* New York: Wadsworth.

French, J. R. P., & Raven, B. (1959). The bases of social power. In D. Cartwright (Ed.), *Studies in social power.* Ann Arbor, MI: Institute for Social Research.

Frost, P., Moore, L., Louis, M., Lundberg, C., & Martin, J. (Eds.). (1991). *Reframing organizational culture.* Beverly Hills, CA: Sage.

Gardner, H., & Krechevsky, M. (1993). *Multiple intelligences: The theory in practice.* New York: Basic Books.

Geier, J. G. (1967). A trait approach to the study of leadership in small groups. *Journal of Communication 17*(4), 316–323.

Gelfand, M. J., Erez, M., & Aycan, Z. (2007). Cross-cultural organizational behavior. *Annual Review of Psychology 58,* 479–514.

Goffman, E. (1959). *The presentation of the self in everyday life.* New York: Anchor.

Goodwin, M. H. (1980). Directive-response speech sequences in girls' and boys' activities. In S. McConnell-Ginet, R. Borker, & N. Furman (Eds.), *Women and language and literature in society* (pp. 157–173). New York. Praeger.

Gray, J., Jr. (1993). *The winning image.* New York: AMACOM.

Gudykunst, W. B., & Ting-Toomey, F. (1988). *Culture and interpersonal communication.* Thousand Oaks, CA: Sage Publications.

Hay, J. (1995). *Gender and humor: Beyond a joke.* New Zealand: Unpublished Master's thesis, Victoria University of Wellington.

Henley, N. (1973–1974). Power, sex, and nonverbal communication. *Berkeley Journal of Sociology 18,* 10–11.

Henley, N. M. (1977). *Body politics.* Greensboro, NC: Spectrum.

Henley, N. M. (1995). Body politics revisited: What do we know today? In P. Kalbfleisch & M. J. Cody (Eds.), *Gender, power, and communication in human relationships* (pp. 27–62). Hillsdale, NJ: Larry Erlbaum Associates.

Henricks, S. H., Kelley, E. A., & Eicher, J. B. (1968). Senior girls' appearance and social acceptance. *Journal of Home Economics 60,* 167–172.

Hensley, W. (1992). Why does the best looking person in the room always seem to be surrounded by admirers? *Psychological Reports 70,* 457–469.

Heritage, J. (1984a). *Garfinkel and ethnomethodology.* Cambridge, England: Polity Press.

Heritage, J. (1984b). The change in state token. In M. Atkinson & J. Heritage (Eds.), *Structures of social action.* Cambridge: Cambridge University Press.

Heritage, J. (2002). The limits of questioning: Negative interrogatives and hostile question content. *Journal of Pragmatics 34,* 1427–1446.

Hickman, G. R. (1998). *Leading organizations: Perspectives for a new era.* London: Sage.

Hofstede, G. (1980). *Culture's consequences: International differences in work-related values.* Beverly Hills, CA: Sage.

Holmes, J. (1995). *Women, men and politeness.* New York, NY: Longman.

Holmes, J. (2000). Politeness, power and provocation: How humor functions in the workplace. *Discourse Studies 2*(2), 159–185.

Holmes, J. (2006). Sharing a laugh: Pragmatic aspects of humor and gender in the workplace. *Journal of Pragmatics 38,* 26–50.

Holmes, J., & Marra, M. (2002). Over the edge? Subversive humor between colleagues and friends. *Humor 15*(1), 65–87.

Holmes, J., & Marra, M. (2004). Leadership and managing conflict in meetings. *Pragmatics 14*(4), 439–462.

Holmes, J., & Marra, M. (2006). Humor and leadership style. *Humor 19*(2), 119–138.

Holmes, J., & Stubbes, M. (2003). "Feminine" workplaces: Stereotype and reality. In J. Holmes & M. Meyerhoff (Eds.), *The handbook of language and gender* (pp. 573–599). Oxford: Blackwell.

Holmes, J., Stubbe, M., & Marra, M. (2003). Language, humor, and ethnic identity marking in New Zealand English. *ASNEL Papers, 7* (pp. 431–455). The politics of English as a world language: New horizones in cultural studies.

Holmes, J., Stubbe, M., & Vine, B. (1999). Constructing professional identity: "Doing power" in policy units. In S. Sarangi & C. Roberts (Eds.), *Talk, work and institutional power: Discourse in medical, mediation and management settings* (pp. 351–385). Berlin: Mouton de Gruyter.

House, R. J. (1976). A 1976 theory of charismatic leadership. In J. G. Hunt & L. L. Larson (Eds.), *Leadership: The cutting edge* (pp. 189–207). Carbondale, IL: Southern Illinois University Press.

House, R. J., Hanges, P. J., Javidan, M., Dorfman, P. W., & Gupta, V. (Eds.). (2004). *Culture, leadership, and organizations: The GLOBE study of 62 societies.* Thousand Oaks, CA: Sage Publications.

Hui, C. H., & Tan, C. K. (1996). Employee motivation and attitudes in the Chinese workforce. In M. H. Bond (Ed.), *The handbook of Chinese psychology* (pp. 364–378). Hong Kong: Oxford University Press.

Hui, C. H., & Triandis, H. C. (1986). Individualism-collectivism: A study of cross-cultural research. *Journal of Cross-cultural Psychology 17*, 225–248.

Jacobs, S. (2002). Maintaining neutrality in third-party dispute mediation. *Journal of Pragmatics 34*, 1403–1426.

James, D., & Drakich, J. (1993). Understanding gender differences in amount of talk: A critical review of research. In D. Tannen (Ed.), *Gender and conversational interaction* (pp. 281–312). New York: Oxford University Press.

Javidan, M., Dorfman, P. W., de Luque, M. S., & House, R. J. (2006). In the Eye of the beholder: Cross cultural lessons in leadership from project GLOBE. *The Academy of Management Perspectives 20*(1), 67–90.

Jenkins, R. (1996). *Social identity.* London: Routledge.

Jian, G., Schmisseur, A. M., & Fairhurst, G. T. (2008). Organizational discourse and communication: The progeny of Proteus. *Discourse and Communication 2*, 299–320.

Johnstone, B. (2002). *Discourse analysis.* Malden, MA: Blackwell Publishers.

Jourard, S. M. (1968). *Disclosing man to himself.* Princeton, NJ: Van Nostrand.

Jourard, S. M., & Rubin, J. E. (1968). Self-disclosure and touching: A study of two modes of interpersonal encounter and their inter-relation. *Journal of Humanistic Psychology 8*, 39–48.

Kakavá, C. (2002). Opposition in modern Greek discourse. *Journal of Pragmatics 34*, 1537–1568.

Kangasharju, H. (2002). Alignment in disagreement. *Journal of Pragmatics 34*, 1447–1472.

Kaplan, R. M. (1978). Is beauty talent? Sex interaction in the attractiveness Halo Effect. *Sex Roles 4*, 195–204.

Kaufmann, A. (2002). Negation prosody in British English. *Journal of Pragmatics 34*, 1473–1494.

Kendall, S. (2003). Creating gender demeanors of authority at work and at home. In J. Holmes & M. Meyerhoff (Eds.), *The handbook of language and gender* (pp. 600–623). Oxford: Blackwell.

Knapp, M. L., & Hall, J. A. (1992). *Nonverbal communication in human interaction* (3rd Ed.). Fort Worth: Harcourt Brace Jovanovich.

Knights, D. & Wilmott, H. (1992). Conceptualizing leadership processes: A study of senior managers in a financial services company. *Journal of Management Studies 29*, 761–782.

Kotthoff, H. (1996). Impoliteness and conversational joking: On relational politics. *Folia Linguistica 30*, 299–327.

Kotthoff, H. (1999). Coherent keying in conversational humour: Contextualising joint fictionalisation. In W. Bublitz, U. Lenk, & E. Ventola (Eds.), *Coherence in spoken and written discourse* (pp. 125–150). Amsterdam/Philadelphia: John Benjamins.

Kotter, J. P. (1990). *A force for change: How leadership differs from management.* New York, NY: Free Press.

Larrain, J. (1979). *The concept of ideology.* London: Hutchinson.

Macionis, J. J., & Gerber, L. M. (2010). *Sociology* (7th Canadian Edition). Don Mills, ONT: Pearson Education Canada.

Modaff, D., & DeWine, S. (2002). *Organizational communication, foundations, challenges, misunderstandings.* Los Angeles: CA: Roxbury.

Mullany, L. (2007). *Gendered discourse in the professional workplace.* London: Palgrave MacMillan.

Neuhauser, P., Bender, R., & Stromberg, K. (2000). *Culture.com: Building corporate culture in the connected workplace.* Toronto: John Wiley and Sons.

Nichols, R., & Stevens, L. (1983). Are you listening? *Language Arts 60*(2), 163–165.

O'Keefe, B. J. (1988). The logic of message design: Individual differences in reasoning about communication. *Communication Monographs 55*, 80–103.

O'Keefe, B. J. (1991). Message design logic and the management of multiple goals. In K. Tracy (Ed.), *Understanding face-to-face intentions: Issues linking goals and discourse* (pp. 131–150). Mahwah, NJ: Erlbaum.

O'Keefe, B. J. (1992a). Developing and testing rational models of message design. *Human Communication Research 18*, 637–649.

O'Keefe, B. J. (1992b). Variation, adaptability, and functional explanation in the study of message design. In G. Philipsen (Eds.), *Developing communication theories* (pp. 85–118). Albany, NY: State University of New York Press.

O'Reilly, C. A., III, Chatman, J., & Caldwell, D. F. (1993). People and organizational culture: A profile comparison approach to assessing person-organization fit. *Academy of Management Journal 34*, 487–516.

Parry, K., & Proctor-Thomson, S. (2003). Leadership, culture and performance: The case of the New Zealand public sector. *Journal of Change Management 3*(4), 376–399.

Pellegrini, E. K., & Scandura, T. A. (2008). Paternalistic leadership: A review and agenda for future research. *Journal of Management 34*(3), 566–593.

Pellegrini, E. K., Scandura, T. A., & Jayaraman, V. (2010). Cross-cultural generalizability of paternalistic leadership: An expansion of leader-member exchange theory. *Group & Organization Management 35*(4), 391–420.

Rahim, A., & Bonoma, T. V. (1979). Managing organizational conflict: A model for diagnosis and intervention. *Psychological Reports 44*, 1325–1344.

Robbins, S. P. (2001). *Organizational behavior.* Upper Saddle River, NJ: Prentice-Hall, Inc.

Robinson, V. M. J. (2001). Embedding leadership in task performance. In K. Wong & C. W. Evers (Eds.), *Leadership for quality schooling* (pp. 90–102). London: Routledge/Falmer.

Rudman, L. A., & Glick, P. (2001, Winter). Prescriptive gender stereotypes and backlash toward agentic women. *Journal of Social Issues 57*(4), 743–762.

Sacks, H. (1984). Notes on methodology. In J. M. Atkinson & J. Heritage (Eds.), *Structures of social action: Studies in conversation analysis* (pp. 2–27). Cambridge, England: Cambridge University Press.

Sacks, H. (1986). On the analyzability of stories by children. In J. J. Gumperz & D. Hymes (Eds.), *Directions in sociolinguistics: The ethnography of communication* (pp. 325–345). Oxford, England: Basil Blackwell.

Sacks, H., Schegloff, E. A., & Jefferson, G. (1974). A simplest systematics for the organization of turn-taking for conversation. *Language 50*, 696–735.

Salopek, J. (1999). Is anyone listening? Listening skills in the corporate setting. *Training and Development 53*, 58–59.

Sandberg, S. (2013). *Lean in: Women, work, and the will to lead.* New York: Alfred A. Knopf.

Sarros, J. C., & Santora, J. C. (2001). Leaders and values: A cross-cultural study. *Leadership & Organization Development Journal 22*(5), 243–248.

Schegloff, E. (1980). Preliminaries to preliminaries: "Can I ask you a question?" *Sociological Inquiry 50*, 104–152.

Schegloff, E., & Sacks, H. (1973). Opening up closings. *Semiotica 8*, 289–327.

Schein, E. (1992). *Organizational culture and leadership* (2nd Ed.). San Francisco: Jossey-Bass.

Schnurr, S. (2009). *Leadership discourse at work: Interactions of humour, gender, and workplace culture.* London: Palgrave MacMillan.

Seckman, M., & Couch, C. (1989). Jocularity, sarcasm, and relationships. *Journal of Contemporary Ethnography 18*(3), 327–344.

Shedletsky, L. J. (1989). The mind at work. In L. J. Shedletsky (Ed.), *Meaning and mind: An intrapersonal approach to human communication.* ERIC and The Speech Communication Association.

Shotter, J. (1993). *Conversational realities: Constructing life through language.* London: Sage.

Sigman, S. J. (1992). Do social approaches to interpersonal communication constitute a contribution to communication theory? *Communication Theory 2*, 347–356.

Slater, P. E. (1966). Role differentiation in small groups. In A. P. Hare, E. F. Borgatta, & R. F. Bales (Eds.), *Small groups: Studies in social interaction* (pp. 610–647). New York, NY: Knopf.

Snyder, M. (1974). Self-monitoring of expressive behavior. *Journal of Personality and Social Psychology 30*, 526–537.

Snyder, M., & Gangestad, S. (2000). Self-monitoring: Appraisal and reappraisal. *Psychological Bulletin 126*(4), 530–555.

Stein, R. T., & Heller, T. (1979). An empirical analysis of the correlations between leadership status and participation rates reported in the literature. *Journal of Personality and Social Psychology 37*, 1993–2002.

Svennevig, J. (2008). Exploring leadership conversations. *Management Communication Quarterly 21*(4), 529–536.

Tannen, D. (1990). *You just don't understand: Women and men in conversation.* New York, NY: Ballantine Books.

Tannen, D. (1994). *Talking from 9 to 5. Women and men in the workplace: Language, sex and power.* New York: Avon.

Taylor, L. C., & Compton, N. H. (1968). Personality correlates of dress conformity. *Journal of Home Economics 60*, 653–656.

Triandis, H. (1990). Cross-cultural studies of individualism and collectivism. In J. Berman (Ed.), *Cross-cultural perspectives* (pp. 41–133). Lincoln, NE: University of Nebraska Press.

Vine, B., Holmes, J., Marra, M., Pfeifer, D., & Jackson, B. (2008). Exploring co-leadership talk through interactional sociolinguistics. *Leadership 4*(3), 339–360.

Walker, R., & Aritz, J. (2014). Leading multicultural teams: A discursive leadership approach. *Journal of Business Communication 51*(1).

Wang, W., Parker, K., & Taylor, P. (2013). *Breadwinner moms: Mothers are the sole or primary provider in four-in-ten households with children; public conflicted about the growing trend.* Retrieved August 1, 2013, from Pew Research Social and Demographic Trends: http://www.pewsocialtrends.org/2013/05/29/breadwinner-moms/

Weinrauch, J., & Swanda, J. (1975). Examining the significance of listening: An exploratory study of contemporary management. *Journal of Business Communication 13*, 25–32.

Wenger, E. (1998). *Communities of practice: Learning, meaning, and identity.* Cambridge: Cambridge University Press.

Widgery, R. N. (1974). Sex of receiver and physical attractiveness of source as determinants of initial credibility perception. *Western Speech 38*, 13–17.

Yamada, H. (1992). *American and Japanese business discourse: A comparison of interactional styles.* Norwood, NJ: Ablex Publishing Corporation.

Yarwood, D. L. (1995). Humor and administration: A serious inquiry into unofficial organizational communication. *Public Administration Review 55*(1), 81–90.

Yoder, J. D. (2001, Winter). Making leadership work more effectively for women. *Journal of Social Issues 57*(40), 815–828.

Yoder, J. D., & Kahn, A. S. (2003). Making gender comparisons more meaningful: A call for more attention to social context. *Psychology of Women Quarterly 27*(4), 281–290.

Yukl, G., & Van Fleet, D. D. (1992). Theory and research on leadership in organizations. In M. D. Dunnette & L. M. Hough (Eds.), *Handbook of industrial & organizational psychology* (2nd ed., Vol. 3) (p. 150). Palo Alto, CA: Consulting Psychologists Press.

Index

Lightning Source UK Ltd.
Milton Keynes UK
UKHW02191411121
393812UK00010B/2143

9 781606 497081